MANIFESTING
HEAVEN

PETER J. NASH

MANIFESTING HEAVEN

Copyright © 2011 by Peter Nash

ISBN: 978-1-77069-280-0

Printed in Canada

Word Alive Press
131 Cordite Road, Winnipeg, MB R3W 1S1
www.wordalivepress.ca

Library and Archives Canada Cataloguing in Publication

Nash, Peter J., 1952-
    Manifesting heaven / Peter Nash.

ISBN 978-1-77069-280-0

    1. Kingdom of God. 2. Spiritual life--Christianity. 3. Christian life. I. Title.

BT94.N38 2011   231.7'2   C2011-903259-7

TABLE OF CONTENTS

FOREWORD

Pastor Peter's revelation of the manifest presence of the Lord and His presence in our being gives us the victory He so richly purchased for us through the cross. Jesus walked in the supernatural, and every believer, every minister of the Gospel, and every church should expect this to be the normal Christian life.

Peter has revealed to us through this book that we have a real adversary and that we wrestle not against flesh and blood. The sooner we realize that our wrestling is not with humanity but is totally spiritual in nature, the easier our daily walk with Him will be. As spirit-led believers, we should always be proactive for the things of God and not reactionary to circumstances or situations. John 10:10 tells us that the enemy's mandate is to kill, rob, and destroy, but Christ has come to give us life more abundantly.

Peter writes from the Spirit of God's perspective and out of that he has gained a revelation. This revelation will be revolutionary for some and their established mindsets. A line has been drawn in the sand, and if you are not totally filled with the Holy Spirit you will not be able to cross over the line into the realms that the Lord collectively has for us.

This book gives people hope and an opportunity to live daily in His presence, in the supernatural, with signs, wonders, and miracles following their lives.

PASTOR CLAUDIO FREIDZON
King of Kings Church
Buenos Aires, Argentina

CHAPTER ONE

Why the Presence of the
Lord Is So Important

How does one go about writing a book on manifesting heaven when so much of the Christian community is so far removed from the reality of heaven on earth? I believe that there is an untapped flow of the Holy Spirit becoming available to those who truly are after the Lord Jesus Christ. This flow will be unprecedented, something not seen since the early church age, and it is becoming available to us for the upcoming end time harvest. The end of the age is virtually upon us and there will be a bride produced without spot or wrinkle.

We live in such exciting times and the Holy Spirit is at work in the hearts and lives of believers. Get ready, as we are about to walk in the reality of the latter half of Galatians 5—totally empowered in the attributes of the Holy Spirit and the Lord Jesus. Our mandate will be to see the presence of the Lord operating in every single life.

I believe in the fullness of being a Christian. You might be asking, what does that mean? It means that more than just a few believers will be utilized to advance the kingdom of God. Rather, each and every one called by His name will have a strong part to play in manifesting a heavenly realm here on earth.

Christianity is about being a believer from the front of the church to the very back row of the church and out the door, pouring onto the streets of our cities. We are called to live out our Christian walk literally in every place our feet tread upon. Christianity is not about your problems or the issues of life; these will take care of themselves when your focus is directed upwards on your risen Saviour. Christianity is about the victory that comes through your problems. Being a Christian doesn't mean you will not face interesting challenges and predicaments; these things will come, but isn't it good to know that you have something greater than those people on the street today?

Christians have a hope within that defies all natural understanding. There is a realm we can draw upon that transcends all our natural senses. Jesus instructed His disciples in the perfect prayer with the words, *"Thy kingdom come. Thy will be done in earth, as it is in heaven"* (Matthew 6:10, KJV). This book is focused on the reality of heaven in our lives. I believe that because there have been forerunners in this earthly realm, the realities of the kingdom will be available to those of the end time generation. In other words, the kingdom will be available to you and every believer.

Some people will wake up hung-over today, and at one time you may have been like that. Isn't God good? He didn't leave you where you were at; He took you from where you were. Isn't that an exciting thought? Why? Because there is a heavenly call upon your life. I understand that you may still struggle with issues of sin, but there is a heavenly reality that flows from the throne room of His grace which will become your perfect enabler. Christianity is a work in process, and the Lord is doing a good work! In order for this to happen, the presence of the Lord is so important. Believe me, it is available to you. It is quite literally already within you.

On February 7, 2010, an incredibly anointed young man named Brandt Trimble was preaching at the church where I was pastor. I was watching the service over live webstream outside the lounge of the hotel we were vacationing at in a Mexican resort. You may be asking, why the lounge? This happened to be the only place I was able to receive an internet connection at the hotel. We were in a warm, open environment looking out on the Sea of Cortez. As I was watching the service, people all around me were coming and going, drinking and partying.

Suddenly, two young ladies ran out of the lounge. They were giddy, talking back and forth to each other right in front of me. The sound on my laptop computer wasn't coming through very well, so I had the computer up to my ear trying to hear the service. Then two men came out and it became clear to me why these girls were so giddy.

Right in front of me the foursome started the process of negotiation for that which would take place that evening. I was thinking to myself, *Hello! I am right here. I am watching something spiritual!* I was about to call down hellfire. Then I felt the Lord say to me, "No. You need to see and know something. There is understanding that I need to bring to you." The foursome negotiated some more, and then they started to walk away together. As they walked away, I was still able to hear what was going on. I won't go into details!

The world needs Christ, and it needs Him desperately. I believe the Lord released a mantle that night for the church where I pastor. It came with understanding and I didn't have to meditate on it. It just suddenly hit me.

The Lord placed a scripture on my heart found in Genesis 4. This scripture had been on my mind for the past eight to ten years. I have tried to wrap my mind around how a generation could be removed from the Garden, removed from perfection, and removed from being in the presence of God. How could they possibly enter into sin? I am talking about Cain and Abel. Or for that matter, how could Adam and Eve have walked away from the Lord?

I asked the Lord for understanding on this. Perhaps you have asked yourself the same question at one time or another. We may be multiple generations removed from the Garden, but the Lord has still called us to a Garden experience with Him. You were made for total communion and fellowship with the creator of the universe. His plans and purposes have never changed for humanity. The question is when—when will this be achieved? I believe the end time generation will experience such a realm that will draw all men unto Him (see John 12:32).

> In the course of time Cain brought some of the fruits of the soil as an offering to the Lord. But Abel brought fat portions from some of the firstborn of his flock. The Lord looked with favor on Abel and his offering, but on Cain and his offering he did not look with favor. So Cain was very angry, and his face was downcast.
>
> Then the Lord said to Cain, "Why are you angry? Why is your face downcast? If you do what is right, will

you not be accepted? But if you do not do what is right, sin is crouching at your door; it desires to have you, but you must master it."

Now Cain said to his brother Abel, "Let's go out to the field." And while they were in the field, Cain attacked his brother Abel and killed him. (Genesis 4:3–8, NIV).

Why is this scripture significant to the presence of the Lord in our lives? Sin is the very instrument that prevents us from walking in not only the revelation of the Lord but His very presence here on earth. Can you remove sin from your own life? Absolutely not, but if we confess our sin He is faithful to forgive us and cleanse us from all unrighteousness, which allows us free access to everything He has for us. The realm of heaven is available to us by the Spirit of the Lord. Let there be a new flow of His presence in your life today. Simply enter in by the Spirit that has been so richly extended to you.

Enemy at the Gate

At one time, I thought there were three types of thoughts in our minds all vying for attention at the same time—God's thoughts, my thoughts, and the devil's thoughts. After my experience at the hotel, I realized that there are only two types of thoughts—God's thoughts and wrong thoughts directly in opposition to God. It may be a good thought, but if it is not God's thought then it is still wrong.

There is a constant battle between God's thoughts and wrong thoughts. The enemy is always at the gates, and the Lord is asking us to choose His thoughts. This is the key. It can't be taught. It can only be captured by the Spirit of the Lord. There are so many wrong thoughts that come into our minds. As Christians, we are in the process of becoming like Jesus. Why does the Word say to pray that you will have understanding, pray that you will have wisdom, and pray that you will have the mind of Christ? Whether you like it or not, you have a mind and there is a battle raging over your mind.

Choices to Make

In Genesis 4, there was a battle going on between Cain and the mandate of heaven. There are constant battles raging in our minds between heavenly thoughts and other thoughts intent on pulling us away from His purposes. Through these battles the Lord is saying, "You have some choices to make." Some of the reasoning behind your choices may be wrong, and some of your thinking is not God's thinking. As a matter of fact, you must check every motivation of your heart to find out whether or not it is rooted in Christ at that particular moment. If not, then you need to ask the Lord for His grace to walk in His plans and purposes.

Our hearts are incredibly complicated. They will lie to us and justify ungodly behaviour and action that does not line up with the Word of God. I point this out because it is so important that we follow after the presence of God. When we have the presence of God, our thought life will start to flow from heaven. Thinking wrong is only part of the sin.

There was a big difference in the offerings that were brought to the Lord from Cain and Abel. One offering had blood in it and the other offering came from the fruit of Cain's labour. Without going into the details, which in itself would require a complete book, the Lord was looking for an offering that required blood. In Genesis 4, God shows that He is so gracious and merciful to those not deserving mercy. When

Cain gave the wrong offering, God went to Cain and reminded him out of love instead of saying that he had messed up. This is the mercy of God. He only corrects those He loves.

Cain became angry with God for bringing him correction and unleashed that anger on his brother. Has this ever happened to you? We don't often like correction, because it that we are wrong. It offends our hearts to be corrected. Cain didn't like God's reaction, and because of this he allowed sin to enter in, resulting in anger and ultimately the death of Abel.

Have you ever heard of the principle of cause and effect? If you speed, you will likely get a speeding ticket at some point, because there is a law in place making speeding illegal. This is a simple example of cause and effect. When we break the law, there are consequences. Cain fell into sin because he had brought the wrong offering and couldn't handle the correction that God brought to him. Sin is sin to God. When the Lord tries to correct you, your response is so very important.

Why did God say that there was no one like David? David committed murder, slept with another man's wife, and did some pretty heavy stuff in anyone's eyes. Still, God said there was no one like him. Why? Because when he was corrected, he would respond by saying, "Against you, Lord, I have sinned." Sin is always against God and will always prevent the kingdom of heaven from manifesting in your life—until you make it right with the Lord.

In one of our services, I once made a comment that all death is related to sin. As a result of that passing statement, a lady who was in attendance became angry with me, because her mother had died. She told me that her mother had been a great, God-loving person. I said to her, "I have no doubt that she was a great Godly woman. Regardless, we have all sinned and we are all going to die." Scripture is clear that sickness and death are totally related to sin. I am not trying to offend you, but it is a reality. We need to understand this principle in scripture. All sin is related to death, and all death is related to sin.

I would like to be like Enoch, and have the Lord take me. If He did it for one, He can do it for others. We like to put God in a box, thinking that if it only happened to one person then it can't happen to us. Who is to say that we can't claim it for ourselves? I want a relationship with God that allows me to walk with Him out of the flow of His presence. I know that day is coming soon for many believers, and this will be a common occurrence. It is so important not to let your natural unsanctified thinking prevent you from experiencing more of God. If He did it once, and He can do it again. Don't let your natural realm influence the supernatural realm. Always remember that the unseen realm is more real than the seen, not the other way around.

Have you ever been angry and asked yourself, *Why am I angry?* While vacationing, I once got so angry that I almost punched someone out. I had my grandbaby Benjamin with me, and at the time he was only three months old. He had been crying and I was carrying him down a long hallway where sounds were much louder than normal. We happened to pass a young man who gave me a dirty look, which I assumed was because of my crying grandson. Completely out of nowhere, a rage came on me and I almost dropped Benjamin. I immediately wanted to punch this guy in the face. I quickly caught myself and said, "Lord, forgive me." There is such a thing as holy anger, but I don't think that was it.

We often make assumptions about others that we have no business making. The Word says we should sow mercy rather than judgement.

My heart's cry is that mercy will prevail. Anger comes from sin, and sin is disobedience to God, no matter how we rationalize it. This is why we become sad, depressed, and angry. There is a spiritual battle raging around us and it is intended to remove us as spiritually significant forces for the kingdom of heaven. With understanding comes light, so walk in the light today. You may be headed in the right direction, but sin is sin. When you choose to sin, there are consequences. However, there is forgiveness to point you back in the right direction.

Sin Crouches at the Door

> If you do what is right, will you not be accepted? But
> if you do not do what is right, sin is crouching at your
> door; it desires to have you, but you must master it.
> (Genesis 4:7, NIV)

Sin crouches at your door. Have you ever been confronted by sin? The reality is that sin is out there and quite literally surrounds us, much like heaven surrounds us. Sin is what caused the fall in the Garden when the devil appeared on the scene.

Ultimately sin is what prevents us from the presence of God. As you draw near to God, He will draw near to you. That is the general philosophy with which I live my life. Therefore, a large percentage of my time is spent by getting to know Him in my life. You draw near by eliminating everything that exalts itself against the knowledge of God. Eliminating the competition for God in your life can only be in and through the Holy Spirit. The Lord is the only one who can work this out for you. He simply asks that you have a humble, willing, and obedient heart.

This is a reality of the kingdom of heaven, a reality we can never lose sight of. When we are disobedient to God, separation from the Lord begins to manifest around us—portals open in our lives and we can slip out into the world. It is for this reason that Christ came to set us free from the law of sin and death (see Romans 8:2). Check your heart regularly to ensure that your motives are in alignment with His motives. You can have Godly portals, and ungodly portals. When you sin, you can enter into one of these ungodly portals. Cain was not being influenced by the Spirit of the Lord but an ungodly Spirit in opposition to God.

Understand that spiritual forces are at work continually around you. According to the Bible, people perish because of a lack of knowledge (see Hosea 4:6). Don't fall into this lack-of-knowledge crowd. Those people I saw in the hotel lounge were under something ungodly, and the Lord showed it to me. That is what sin does to our lives; it brings us out of Godly portals and into something that is not of the Lord. It happens when we make ungodly choices, and no one from this realm is exempt of being pulled to and fro in our relationship with the Lord. Sometimes we wonder why it is happening. We need to put it into perspective and try seeing it the way God sees it, through the eyes of His Spirit. When you do, heaven on Earth will open up to you in a very real and discernable way. This is about walking in the here and now, totally infused by heaven. It is about God showing us how to walk in a realm that is available to each and every one of us. Choose His life today, which is free from sin. *"So if the Son sets you free, you will be free indeed"* (John 8:36, NIV).

Our carnal nature is in direct opposition to the Lord. It is crouching at the door, ready to pounce when you walk away from the obedience of

God in your life. Both Cain and Abel had the revealed truth of the Lord, but it was Abel who chose to walk in it. There was something in him that was different from Cain. Much like others that would follow after him, he was indeed of a different spirit, which is how the Lord referred to Caleb and Joshua in later years.

If something has been made available even to just one person, it is available to you and me. Set your sights on a higher realm. There is a different Spirit that you can draw upon, and that is the Spirit of the Lord, who changes and predisposes you to walk in a Godly realm of His supernatural glory. There is coming a day when the whole earth *"will be filled with the knowledge of the glory of the Lord, as the waters cover the sea"* (Habakkuk 2:14, NIV). Could the time of the release of His glory be upon us? I submit that it is coming quickly, and it is available for you.

Why is the presence of God so important? Simple—it keeps you from sin, because those who love Christ obey His commandments. Avoiding sin is only possible through the Lord Jesus Christ, His love in operation in your life, and the power of the Holy Spirit. The Lord said to Cain, *"You must master it"* (Genesis 4:7, NIV). In our own strength, this task would be impossible; however, it is made possible by the Spirit of the Lord. The Lord is also calling us to master this. Yes, there will continually be a war going on in our earthly vessel, but you can walk in His dominion. It was a test for Cain, and it is a test for you and me. Choose His life.

How Does Sin Start?

> Now Cain said to his brother Abel, "Let's go out to the field." And while they were in the field, Cain attacked his brother Abel and killed him. (Genesis 4:8, NIV)

Sin starts purposely and, whether you like to think this or not, we choose to sin. It starts as a thought. It may be a small thought. That is how it begins. Sin entered the Garden through a planted thought that somehow God had not told Adam and Eve the truth. Then, desire for something not to be touched was planted in Eve's heart. Desire flows out of our emotional realm—or soul. As beings with free will, we must always be making choices in our lives. When faced with choices between light and darkness, I believe the Holy Spirit empowers us to walk through His grace in a Godly way. Once sin is chosen, it sears our conscience. Our conviction to walk away from sin becomes weaker and weaker, unless we break the sin cycle through repentance. This is your part. God's part is to forgive us and cleanse us from all unrighteousness, but we have to repent. Sin will harden your heart to heavenly realities, opening the door to unbelief about God's goodness towards you.

This is exactly what happened to Eve in the Garden. Every time you sin, a portal opens, giving sin access into your life. You might be having troubles with finances or relationships. If so, ask yourself if you are walking in Godly principles for your finances and relationships. If your heart is honest and you are not walking in His principles, simply repent and let Him work in your life. Engage heaven on your side and see heavenly results. Godly principles produce Godly results. Cain fell into sin, and unless he repented he couldn't have done anything else. Repentance simply means asking the Lord for forgiveness and going in the opposite direction through the help of the Holy Spirit. It may not be the easy way, but it most definitely is the highway toward abundant life.

The Perfect Prayer

When the disciples asked Jesus about the right way to pray, Jesus introduced the perfect prayer. Part of the prayer goes like this: *"Thy kingdom come. Thy will be done in earth, as it is in heaven"* (Matthew 6:10, KJV). You are called to a heavenly environment and a heavenly realm of His glory. That heavenly environment isn't in the "sweet by and by." I believe that if Christ gave us a prayer to pray, this is it. The perfect prayer. If He gave us the prayer, then I believe it is available. If it wasn't, why give it to us?

Remember, the Lord was all about releasing others to achieve what He had achieved. He said that He had to go in order to release the Comfort—the Holy Spirit—in order that the work of Christ would continue on the earth through His chosen vessels, you and me (John 16:7). When you understand this, you will understand that heaven on earth is truly available to us. There is a realm of glory that you can walk in by the Spirit. That heavenly environment is for you today.

A lot of Christians can't get their minds around this, which is precisely the problem, because spiritual principles can never be intellectually discerned; they must simply be accepted by faith, which is an unseen principle. When Jesus says we can have heaven on earth, I believe it! We may not have it at this moment, but we need to accept that it is available for us. That is why we need the presence of the Lord Jesus Christ in our lives. In spending time with Him in His presence, we begin to have our hearts and lives regenerated by the Holy Spirit.

How Do We Get Revelation?

Revelation comes through the presence of God in operation in your life. It flows out of an intimate relationship with the Lord and His communion with you. This is why the presence is so important. I ask for revelation from the Lord all the time, for without revelation the Bible is simply written words on a page with no spiritual significance. When the revealed truth of those words hit your heart and life, they have power, and all heaven stands behind them. If I am not flowing out of revelation, I am flowing through the natural, which produces natural results. I am after supernatural results in every area of my life. It is important to minimize our natural experience by maximizing our spiritual experience. You can do this by purposefully spending time with the Lord, like you would with a close friend. Put aside the busyness of life, and all your cares and concerns, and simply spend quality time with Him.

Yes, we are three-part beings—spirit, soul, and body—so let your spirit be in charge, the way the Lord intended from the beginning. To walk under a manifested heaven, we need to be completely led by our Spirit, bearing witness to the Spirit of the Lord in us.

I get goose bumps when I speak on this subject. Some of us are satisfied where we are at right now, but there is so much more available to those who believe. Some say, "Well, we won't go any further, so let's not get too fanatical." I really do not believe there will be anyone so fanatical that they overshoot heaven, but there is a real potential to undershoot heaven! My advice is to aim high—higher than where you are right now. You definitely will not overshoot heaven.

Some circles of Christians say, "I get a hundred bucks a week and I have food on the table." They believe they are happy, and that's all there is. Someday they will die and meet their maker. I can categorically tell you that you can meet your maker each and every day and really experience what it means to have heaven on earth in fulfillment to the perfect prayer. We need to realize that there is so much more available to those who believe. A hunger and thirst is developing like never before in the lives of believers. A manifested heaven will bring a revelation of mysteries and secrets hidden for the end of the ages, which is upon us. The Lord knows all of our needs, and if you ask for revelation you will receive it. Many times, I have looked at a certain portion of scripture over and over again with no real understanding of it. Suddenly, in the power of the Holy Spirit, revelation hits and that scripture becomes life to me. The timing of the Lord is so perfect when you are in Him!

> But seek first his kingdom and his righteousness, and all these things will be given to you as well. (Matthew 6:33, NIV)

In this scripture, if you don't know what "all" means, it means everything. It means your healing, financial victory, and walking in the supernatural. I am after the realm of the supernatural in everything I do. Do you need more supernatural on your natural? You can have it by the Spirit of the Lord.

Not everyone has arrived. If you have that impression, you are wrong. Life is a journey, and it is a process to get everything that God has for your life. It is available and has always been available to those who believe. A heavenly invasion has already taken place for you. Lord, I desire your realm of glory in operation in my life, totally encapsulated by the atmosphere of heaven. Rest in the midst of storms, singing praises to the Most High, like Paul and Silas in the Book of Acts. They were in prison and when an earthquake of the Spirit hit; chains fall off and the gatekeepers were set free. A manifested heavenly invasion will demonstrate the Gospel with chains falling off and lives being set free.

Being Sifted Like Grain

> Simon, Simon (Peter), listen! Satan has asked excessively that [all of] you be given up to him [out of the power and keeping of God], that he might sift [all of] you like grain, but I have prayed especially for you [Peter], that your [own] faith may not fail; and when you yourself have turned again, strengthen and establish your brethren. And [Simon Peter] said to Him, Lord, I am ready to go with You both to prison and to death. (Luke 22:31–33)

This scripture describes Jesus after the last supper taking His disciple Peter aside. Jesus spoke and said, "Listen." When Jesus speaks, we need to listen. He said, *"Satan has asked excessively that [all of] you be given up to him [out of the power and keeping of God], that he might sift [all of] you like grain."* If we are disciples of the Lord Jesus, this is going to happen to each of us in a unique way. We are all going to be sifted like grain. The Lord Jesus specifically prayed for Peter in this scripture, and He has specifically prayed for all of us. He walked in perfect communion with the Father, and He knew exactly what was going on. The faith of the Lord Jesus Christ will not fail. A Christian is called to walk as a Christian and to go where the Lord desires for us to go. We most definitely have free will, but at the same time the steps of a righteous man/woman are ordered of Him. We must understand that each step along the course of life may not be that attractive to us, but all steps are beneficial to walking in the heavenly realm.

Sin Must Not Get a Vote

That means you must not give sin a vote in the way you conduct your lives. Don't give it the time of day. Don't even run little errands that are connected with that old way of life. Throw yourselves wholeheartedly and full-time—remember, you've been raised from the dead!—into God's way of doing things. Sin can't tell you how to live. After all, you're not living under that old tyranny any longer. You're living in the freedom of God.

So since we're out from under the old tyranny, does that mean we can live any old way we want? Since we're free in the freedom of God, can we do anything that comes to mind? Hardly. You know well enough from your own experience that there are some acts of so-called freedom that destroy freedom. Offer yourselves to sin, for instance, and it's your last free act. But offer yourselves to the ways of God and the freedom never quits. All your lives you've let sin tell you what to do. But thank God you've started listening to a new master, one whose commands set you free to live openly in his freedom! (Romans 6:12–18, The Message)

Because of the cross, you must not give sin a vote in your life. Have you ever had to take a thought captive? Scripture says we should take captive every thought *"that exalts itself against the knowledge of God"* (2 Corinthians 10:5). Don't give sin a vote! Don't give it a place! This is only possible by the Spirit of the Lord. Some people may call you fanatical, but I believe we need to get more fanatical. The devil is afraid of you, afraid that you will actually make a difference for the kingdom of heaven when you walk under a manifested heaven in your life. You should never let anyone tell you otherwise.

As Christians, we are called to be wholehearted and full-time, not just casual, in our walk. We need God's way of doing things, which will open up a new realm to us. Don't let sin tell you how to live! There is a better way for you. If you are in sin, you are in bondage. That is why it is so important to have the presence of the Lord in your life to walk in a manifested heaven—or open heaven.

CHAPTER TWO

Are You Being Brainwashed
or Manipulated?

Deception

Have you ever seen the movie *The Matrix*? In the film, very few of the characters actually walked in the understanding that they were living in a manufactured state designed to hide who they really were. They were simply living out their lives without understanding that they were walking in the wrong realm.

There are many elements of *The Matrix* that correspond to our lives here on earth. Most of us live on earth not fully aware that there is a purpose in and for our lives, and that we are here to make a difference. We are, in fact, heavenly ordained invaders into the kingdom of darkness. That's what manifesting heaven is all about! We are a force in opposition to the kingdom of darkness. Another interesting observation would be that we are aliens sent to occupy this earth, but through careful manipulation by our adversary we don't see what our actual purpose really is. Our true purpose is to fulfill the works of Christ. Christ said that He had to go in order that the Holy Spirit would come and empower those who believe. Christ also said in John 14 that believers would do greater works than He did upon the earth. I believe that the greater-works generation is about to be released upon the earth as heaven is manifested. If you let Him, you will be part of it.

Deception is constantly trying to enter our lives. Have you ever believed something and found out it was wrong? I have, and I may still have areas that the Holy Spirit desires to work on through the revealed truth of the Gospel.

Up until last year, I had a real dislike of eating eggs. This was not a big deal for God, but it was for me. I refused to eat them, and I was so predisposed to not eating them that I could not understand how anyone else could eat them, either. Suddenly, I decided one day to try an egg omelette, and suddenly I had an egg omelette paradigm shift! Now I make the best omelette in the world. I had been deceived.

We are all deceived from time to time, because our minds have a preconceived ideas about most things. These preconceptions limit the kingdom of heaven from manifesting in our lives. That is why having the mind of Christ is so incredibly important to achieving a manifested-heavenly focus. We must also understand that we are seated with Christ far above principalities, powers, and rulers of darkness. Our position is above issues and concerns. When we pray, it is from a position of authority—not weakness. We are not undercomers but overcomers in Christ. That is a heavenly reality. If we could catch hold of these heavenly principles, our lives would be revolutionized forever.

Something in man desires to, and has always desired to, go his own way. The fall of man—just like the fall of Lucifer—has always been about going our own way and doing our own thing. Many times, we adjust our thinking to match the way we want to go. Take an alcoholic, for example. You cannot tell an alcoholic that they have a problem until they confront the issue and get a revelation that they do, indeed, have an issue. If the issue is not resolved, their lives will be adversely affected, and generations may be adversely effected.

Scripture says that sin follows to the third or fourth generation, but grace goes to the thousandth generation for those who love Him. Call upon the grace of God today which is available for your life. There are issues you are dealing with in your own life that you don't want there— and they may very well be generational. This goes for any addiction. I know the Lord grieves over these things, because He came specifically to set the captives free. Under freedom, you are actually walking in the heavenly realm of glory.

As I write this, I just finished several meetings in Vietnam where the tangible presence of heaven was evident in every meeting. Heaven is real. Whether you agree or not, it can surround you and envelop every part of your being. There is always a degree of deception in humanity preventing us from entering this aspect of His glory. Matthew 18:20 says, *"For where two or more are gathered in my name, there am I in the midst of them"* (NIV). Simply believe the scripture, and heaven will invade your atmosphere.

Deception can be a conscious choice, and we need to have the light of the Gospel shine deep into our hearts, illuminating the deepest recesses in order that we walk in His manifested glory here on earth. The truth lies in the Word of God. Deception falls away the closer we get to God. The Bible says, *"For false christs and false prophets will rise and show great signs and wonders to deceive, if possible, even the elect"* (Matthew 24:24, NKJV). Even the elect can be deceived.

Every issue in life comes down to the motives of the heart. If your motive is right before the Lord, you are positioned for a heavenly invasion in your life. Have you ever heard the comment, "Well, the end justify the means"? That is deception. There were two trees in the Garden of Eden—the Tree of Life and the Tree of the Knowledge of Good and Evil. That tells me that we can do all sorts of good things, but if it doesn't flow from the Tree of Life (the Lord Jesus), we are definitely outside of the heavenly realm. We will get the same results. Even though it was something good, it will be as if it came from something evil, because it did not flow from the Tree of Life. To see heavenly results, our motives must line up to the Lord's plans and purposes. Make it a daily practice to examine your own heart in all things.

I am a retired police officer from the Royal Canadian Mounted Police (RCMP). At one time, I was stationed in Swift Current, Saskatchewan. At about 5:00 one morning, I found myself driving down the Trans-Canada Highway. This is probably one of the longest highways on the face of planet earth. It stretches from one end of our nation to the other. At this time in the morning while on night shift, most of the serious issues of the night had come to an end. I started to relax a little as the sun started to come up over the horizon.

While driving on this highway, I noticed that every car I passed heading in the opposite direction was pulling over and stopping, which I found to be very interesting. I remember checking all of my emergency operation equipment to ensure nothing was on emergency mode, and nothing was. There was a lot of traffic for that time of day and the thought came to me that all these people must be high on something, and I should take immediate action to enforce the laws of the land. I was thinking to myself, *Maybe I should pull over some of these vehicles. They are acting quite strange.*

Suddenly it dawned on me that I was driving the wrong way down this four-lane highway. It wasn't all these others in the wrong—it was actually me. They weren't the strange ones—I was! For a few minutes, I was totally walking in deception, thinking I was right in my driving. Ephesians 1:17–19 says that the eyes of our understanding will be enlightened to see clearly. This scripture tells me that, in fact, we do not see clearly, and we need to pray that we *do* see clearly. When we do see clearly, we will be under a manifested heaven. My thinking was that everyone else was acting weird, when in reality I was the one acting weird. I had been deceived. Praise God for the protection of the Lord and that He can open our spiritual eyes to see.

Scripture says that at the end of the age, the Lord will release mysteries and secrets that have been hidden in His Word. Under a manifested heaven, these mysteries and secrets will be revealed to you. This is what excites me about your destiny; you may not see clearly now, but those who hunger and thirst for Him will see clearly and the spirit of deception will be far from you.

I told the highway story to illustrate a point. We can think we are doing something right and blame others when we should be first looking at ourselves. No one thinks they are being deceived when they are. That is the nature of deception. Deception is defined as a misleading falsehood. Everyone can be deceived. The only criterion is that you think you are right, which most of us do most of the time. Remember to examine your heart in all things and humble yourself, because His grace will be available at that very moment.

All of us, at one point in our lives as believers, needed to receive Christ. The only way to do this is to receive a revelation of salvation from the presence of the Lord. He totally and completely reveals Himself to you, much like the process Peter walked in when he received his revelation of Christ in Luke 22. The same principle applies for your life and for anyone who has truly accepted the Lord Jesus in their life. At the moment of salvation, a manifested heaven was operating in your life.

Being a Christian is so exciting, because a manifested heaven is not only available for your salvation but for every aspect of your life, from the smallest to the largest decision. A manifested heaven is there for you. You went all those years as an unbeliever thinking you were right, which was the same thinking the apostle Paul had until he had a revelation of Christ which transformed his life forever. Under a manifested heaven, decisions are made with forever in mind. At the point of salvation, you met the Lord Jesus Christ and everything changed.

As you get closer to the Lord, deception falls away and you are better able to see the world, though the Spirit of the Lord operating in your life. If you listen to that still small voice of the Lord, your life will change and heaven will invade your life in a new and profound way. You will literally become a new creation and all things will become new in Christ.

One time, I was walking down the stairs in my house. I heard a small voice say, "Hold on to the handrail. You are about to slip." I didn't listen. Guess what? I slipped. Have you ever slipped up in life because you refused to listen to that still small voice? Just a thought, but the Lord is in that still small voice. Quiet yourself enough to listen.

The Way of Man Leads to Death

> There is a way that seems right to a man, but its end is
> the way of death. (Proverbs 14:12 NKJV)

When you think that you are right, examine your heart. If it doesn't line up with God, think again. We fail when we do things because they feel good or look like the best course of action. If they are not rooted in the Lord, they will produce something that neither you nor the Lord desires for your life. Every decision must line up with the Word of God.

So many times, I hear people say, "I feel the need to take this or that course of action." But scripture is often clearly in opposition to the direction they want to proceed in. They deceive themselves into thinking their feelings in some way are more important than the Word of God. Please hear me—the Lord loves you enough to have released His Word—and that Word should be absolute to each of us—yet so many times we allow other things to intervene between us and the Lord. Under all circumstances, you need to be governed by the Word of God. You cannot allow yourself the luxury of being led by your feelings, as your feelings lie to you on an ongoing basis.

It was feelings that caused the downfall of man in the Garden, and feelings have been plaguing humanity ever since. Am I saying all feelings are wrong? Absolutely not, but all feelings must be submitted to the Lord, to see whether it is from Him or not. Then, if they are His feelings, they will produce Godly and heavenly results in your life. We need to be listening for that still small voice in everything we do. *"There is a way that seems right to a man, but its end is the way of death"* (Proverbs 14:12, NKJV).

Have you ever tried to justify your behaviour when you know deep inside that it is not pleasing to the Lord? You say something like, "So and so did this, and so and so did that, so I am justified in doing this." You might not verbally come out and say these words, but it is going on in your mindset whether you understand this principle or not. Another consequence of this line of reasoning is that we sometimes intentionally punish someone for something they have done. We do these sorts of things all the time to one another. Clearly such behaviour closes the window of heaven from operating in our lives. My wife says it like this: "When you have been wounded or offended, move in the opposite spirit." In other words, simply walk in love with everyone all the time. Don't allow your feelings to control you. Thinking we are right without examining our heart will quickly lead to "death."

When we get off-track, there will be markers along the way, so don't ignore that still small voice; listen carefully for the voice of the Lord. Listen for His Spirit. When I was driving the wrong way on that highway, there were markers indicating that I was going the wrong way. I chose to ignore the markers, or I simply didn't see them. Let your eyes be open to see by the Spirit in you. Your destiny depends on it. In the Bible, David, Moses, and Samson all had markers along the way, but for one reason or the other they choose not to listen to them. They chose their own course of action. Remember Proverbs 14:12—*"There is a way that seems right to a man, but its end is the way of death."*

When things come up in your life, there are only two ways to see the big picture—you either have divine discernment from the Lord or you don't. This is why judgment is so wrong. The Lord says, *"For judgment is without mercy to the one who has shown no mercy. Mercy triumphs over judgment"* (James 2:13, NKJV).We see from a human perspective. God sees from a divine perspective, beyond appearances. The Lord judges righteously. We, too, need to judge righteously, with His eyes, to see. As human beings we have prejudices and potential selfish, hidden motives that are not easily discernible, even to ourselves, unless we are led by the Spirit. The motives of our own heart can be unclear unless we ask God. We need to ask ourselves if we are trying to please Him or man. Focusing on changing others over changing ourselves leads to death, which definitely has no place under an open heaven and under the power of the Holy Spirit. Trying to get what you want by manipulating others leads us to death.

Sin Is Sin to God

Only you know if you are justifying ungodly behaviour in your life and in your heart. Actions speak louder than words. You can say one thing, but your actions might tell a different story. Actions always and without fail speak louder than your words. You cannot speak negatively about someone and then say you love that person. This is a contradiction and double-mindedness. Ensure your actions support the words you speak.

I once heard a great quote, but I am unsure who said it. The quote was: "The biggest hurdle to Godliness is somehow attempting to configure God to our own standards, rather than configuring Him to His standard." God is compassionate and full of love; that is His standard. It is not about to change. Walk under His standard, not your own. Sometimes we think that God "winks" at our sin or lack of love for others. For example, some think they are so anointed and Godly that God allows them to get away with certain things in their lives. They think they are somehow a special case. I believe we are all called to a higher standard, empowered by the Holy Spirit. Seek holiness and His righteousness for your life and turn away from all forms of evil.

I do believe that those in ministry should be held to a higher standard. Let me tell you this—God loves you enough to correct you, so do not ignore His voice when He speaks! Sin is sin to God. It's all the same. It doesn't matter if you commit adultery, harbour anger, feel rejected, are under anxiety and pressure, or don't go to church when He clearly asks us to do so in His Word. Sin is simply disobedience to Him. Basically, what I am trying to say is summed up in Proverbs 14:12—*"There is a way that seems right to a man, but its end is the way of death."*

CHAPTER THREE

Breaking out of Cycles

You can be in a summer season with the Lord every day, never being dictated to by your circumstances. This is what propelled the Gospel forward in the New Testament church. Advancement despite opposition is a key to living under a manifested heaven. Many people tend to go from cycle to cycle. When everything is good, they feel good, but when everything is bad, they feel bad. They keep repeating the cycle like the children of Israel in the wilderness. Somehow they get it, but they continue to walk around the mountain just one more time. This pattern continues until they come under a manifested heaven and every challenge becomes an opportunity to see the kingdom of heaven advance in their lives.

They walk around the same mountain over and over. This is the type of atmosphere that I call "outer court Christianity." This basically means you are saved and on your way to heaven but aren't very effective for advancing the kingdom of heaven on earth. In this experience, you are like a house built upon shifting sand instead of the clear foundation of the Lord Jesus Christ. I believe the Lord has released for each of us an inner court experience. I am convinced that the timing of this is now, not tomorrow. Now is the time to enter into an inner court realm of thinking. If you can see it with your spiritual eyes, I believe you can have it. It is there for you, and now in this time.

On December 18, 2009, while leading an early morning prayer service at our church, the Lord Jesus took me into a vision. It was a vision of the tabernacle spoken of in the Book of Exodus. In this vision, I found myself in the outer court. I was quite simply minding my own business, which was significant because I should be minding His business while on earth. All of a sudden, I heard a voice calling my name: "Peter, come over here." As I turned and looked in the direction of the voice, I realized I was staring into the face of the Lord Jesus standing at the entrance to the Holy of Holies. He motioned and called for me to join Him at the entrance to His tent, because He had something to give me.

I won't reveals he details at this point, because what He gave me will be covered in more detail later in this book, but let it suffice for now that each of us has been called to that very same inner court experience. So get ready! If it is available to just one of us, it is available to all of us! If it is available to me, it is available to you.

Whatever the Lord Jesus walked under on this earth, we can also have; this is what a manifested heaven is all about. Notice that Jesus was challenged and opposed because He was manifesting the kingdom of heaven on earth. A manifested heaven and its invasion in and around our lives will always be opposed. Understand this: a manifested heaven is about the destiny of the Lord in your life, and His destiny for you is in opposition to other spiritual forces and worldly influences.

I have a saying that goes like this: "Turmoil around your life means absolutely nothing other than that there is a high degree of probability that you are doing something right for His kingdom, unless of course you are walking in sin." We are called to be a greater-works generation. It says in the Bible, *"Most assuredly, I say to you, he who believes in Me, the works that I do he will do also; and greater works than these he will do, because I go to My Father"* (John 14:12, NKJV). This promise has not fully manifested in our lives, but it is available—and if the Word says it, it will happen.

> The Spirit of the Lord [is] upon Me, because He has anointed Me [the Anointed One, the Messiah] to preach the good news (the Gospel) to the poor; He has sent Me to announce release to the captives and recovery of sight to the blind, to send forth as delivered those who are oppressed [who are downtrodden, bruised, crushed, and broken down by calamity]. (Luke 4:18)

You do not need to be oppressed anymore. I believe there are countless keys in scripture, but you need to personally insert every key in a lock and turn it to unlock the door. I can't do it for you. Here's the deal: the Lord Jesus has already achieved it for your life the moment He said, "It is finished." You have spiritual eyes and the Lord desires that you use them. Circumstances in your life cannot dictate who you are in Christ Jesus. You are positioned in a heavenly realm with Him.

Throughout the years, I have seen people on fire for God who suddenly began to move away from God. They became overwhelmed by circumstances, questioning where the Lord is. Suddenly they were pulled out of their positions in Christ back to being controlled by circumstances. Our focus needs to be getting positioned back to the place He has reserved for us. I know life is not easy at times, and no one is exempt from the attacks of our adversary, but seek always to get back to where He wants you to be, under a manifested heaven. The Lord doesn't move away and He never changes. His position is always the same. His love is unconditional. Life will always have ruts that are hard to get out of, and this may be your challenge, but as Paul said, *"[His] grace is sufficient for [me]"* (2 Corinthians 12:9, NKJV).

Just know that He is with you and will neither leave you nor forsake you. We need to have a lifestyle of honouring the Lord, and be honouring to the Lord in all things. *"Honor the Lord with your possessions, and with the firstfruits of all your increase"* (Proverbs 3:9, NKJV). We need to make a lifestyle of giving and honouring Him in everything we do. Then we can watch and see what He will do. Just do it. The Lord sees this and is honoured.

[For I always pray to] the God of our Lord Jesus Christ, the Father of glory, that He may grant you a spirit of wisdom and revelation [of insight into mysteries and secrets] in the [deep and intimate] knowledge of Him, by having the eyes of your heart flooded with light, so that you can know and understand the hope to which He has called you, and how rich is His glorious inheritance in the saints (His set-apart ones), and [so that you can know and understand] what is the immeasurable and unlimited and surpassing greatness of His power in and

for us who believe, as demonstrated in the working of
His mighty strength. (Ephesians 1:17–19)

I want everything this scripture talks about. If you desire this, you
can have it. You have eyes to see clearly by the Spirit of the Lord.

Issues in life mostly come from blurred sight or being dictated and
distracted by circumstances. My wife Cathryn and I were once coming back from a conference in Dallas, Texas. We had been up very late
at night, and since we had an early flight the next day we arrived at
the airport incredibly exhausted. The line for the check-in counter was
the longest I had ever seen in my travel experience. After about twenty
minutes or so, it became obvious that we would not make our flight,
and at that moment I began to hear the voice of the Lord speaking to
me. Of course, there were other voices, like a fearful voice telling me we
were going to miss our flight and an anxious voice saying we weren't
going to make it.

This is what I heard the Lord saying: "Peter, you can walk in the
natural right now and choose to become frustrated, or you can look up
and see heaven manifest in and around your life."

You see, there is a natural, outer court way for us to do things and
there is an inner court way of doing things. So I chose at that moment
not to become frustrated and decided specifically to do things in a
heavenly way. In other words, I decided to choose the Lord's way of
doing things. Then the Lord said, "Okay, look around and do what I tell
you to do." As I looked, I saw a man in front of me. The Lord directed
me to speak to him. I was able to share the Gospel of the kingdom with
this man who had a completely different non-Christian faith. I planted
what I believe to have been the Lord's seed into his life. Next, the Lord

had me look in the opposite direction, where I struck up a conversation with a couple who turned out to be former pastors. They had been totally devastated in ministry and I had the opportunity to encourage them for an extended period of time. Even though they ended up cancelling our flight, I believe that both of my conversations were ordained by the Lord under a manifested heaven.

It is entirely possible that this was the Lord's plan before the foundations of the world. Of course, the Lord knew that the events of the day would happen as they unfolded. I had the opportunity to buy into the Lord's plans instead of being frustrated by my circumstances. I had a delightful morning full of God, and may I say it was an exhilarating experience! Heaven is waiting for us to buy into His plans and purposes. Don't be afraid to look up. The business of daily life often prevents us from seeing His kingdom at work clearly. We all fall into the trap of just daily walking out our lives on this earth without truly thinking about His kingdom. Trust me, if you apply this principle in your life you will be under a manifested heaven, and I believe you will truly walk in a new era of anticipation of the Lord. There is no life like that of being a believer of the Lord Jesus.

We need to have the lens and filter to see circumstances the Lord has ordained us to be in or allowed into our lives. Have you ever judged circumstances wrong? Let me tell you, this has happened to everyone. Another important key for achieving the promises is found in Matthew 7:7. Ask the Lord, and don't stop asking: *"Ask, and it will be given to you; seek, and you will find; knock, and it will be opened to you"* (NKJV). Answers from the Lord don't always come the way you think, but He still answers prayer.

Love never fails [never fades out or becomes obsolete or comes to an end]. As for prophecy (the gift of interpreting the divine will and purpose), it will be fulfilled and pass away; as for tongues, they will be destroyed and cease; as for knowledge, it will pass away [it will lose its value and be superseded by truth]. (1 Corinthians 13:8)

"Love never fails [never fades out or becomes obsolete or comes to an end]." Love is a gift of the Spirit. Agape love is a gift from God to be released for and through your life, and it always manifests heaven. You may feel like your life is a constant race. Never count God out of the race. Even in the darkest hours, God is always there. He is running with you. You need to have complete communion with the Lord.

And to love Him with all the heart, with all the understanding, with all the soul, and with all the strength, and to love one's neighbor as oneself, is more than all the whole burnt offerings and sacrifices. (Mark 12:33, NKJV)

This should be planted in everyone's heart. Do not hold anything back. Out of the love I have for Him, I am able to flow in love for others. The fullness of the Lord in your life will enable you to love others. He has to be at the centre. Love him first with your heart and soul. If you do this people will start to look at you and say, "You look different... in a good way." Love is the key.

However, we possess this precious treasure [the divine Light of the Gospel] in [frail, human] vessels of earth, that the grandeur and exceeding greatness of the power

may be shown to be from God and not from ourselves.
(2 Corinthians 4:7)

You carry a precious commodity, one that is more precious than gold or silver. The Lord knew what He was doing when He chose you. You were chosen for a specific purpose. He knew He would send you to earth and that there would be a day when you would choose Him. The scripture says, *"Just as He chose us in Him before the foundation of the world, that we should be holy and without blame before Him in love"* (Ephesians 1:4, NKJV). Never lose sight of that. If you want to break out of the cycles in your life, you need to know you are a precious carrier of cargo.

For who has known or understood the mind (the counsels and purposes) of the Lord so as to guide and instruct Him and give Him knowledge? But we have the mind of Christ (the Messiah) and do hold the thoughts (feelings and purposes) of His heart. (1 Corinthians 2:16)

"We have the mind of Christ." The Bible clearly states that we have His mind and *"hold the thoughts of His heart."* Get out of your mind. Go after His. The availability of His mind is not only for the sweet by and by, if we go to heaven or get hit by lightning. If you are in the Lord, you cannot make a mistake. Be led by faith, and not by circumstances or a spirit of fear.

Every year, our church does a camp meeting. It costs anywhere between $120,000 and $150,000. The Lord totally and completely takes care of it. If you hear something from the Lord, you need to do what He says out of nothing else other than a spirit of obedience. The world will be used by the devil to come against you. Well-meaning and well-intended people will oppose you, and it won't be an accident. This happens when you are walking in the Lord's plans and purposes for your life, not despite it. The devil is a loser. He is a defeated foe and he wants you to believe that you, too, are defeated. You need to say, "No, in the name of Jesus."

Not everyone is on your side, and you need to understand this fact. Love everyone, but be very careful who you connect your soul with. Many people want to keep you walking in a lower realm. It's comfortable for them, because they want to remain in a low realm and may not want to go higher with the Lord. Are those around you desirous of becoming more Christ-like in their life? Choose who you associate with carefully. If you make the wrong choice in this area, you will be pulled from your heavenly realm. As the saying goes, misery loves company. You need to walk in a higher realm. The key is to remember that more people are for you than against you, and most believers desire more of the Lord in their life.

> From that time forth Jesus began [clearly] to show His disciples that He must go to Jerusalem and suffer many things at the hands of the elders and the high priests and scribes, and be killed, and on the third day be raised from death. (Matthew 16:21)

Jesus had an assignment. He set His mind and path on His Father. He wasn't moved by anyone. We need to make a point of changing one thing in our lives at a time, by the grace of God. Don't try to take on ten things. This is only between you and the Lord. You need to ask Him for His grace. Set your mind on Christ and go after all He has promised for your life. If you so, everything He was after is available to you.

CHAPTER FOUR

Created in and for the
Glory of the Lord

Heaven on Earth

By the victory of Jesus, we are equipped for everything in life. At the church I pastor, the pulpit has a box with hankies in it should I or anyone ministering have need of one. One service, I asked a young man to open the box for me after I had been trying to open it for what seemed like several minutes. In seconds the box was open and a hankie was in my hand. It showed me that you can have whatever you focus on; he was focused on opening the box, but I was focused on preaching the Word. If you focus on heaven, I believe you can open the portal to heaven for your life. The Lord Jesus achieved this for us. We don't need to wait for a heaven-on-earth experience. We can have it now, by the power of the Holy Spirit. This experience will be unprecedented in the church body when it hits the church, which will suddenly become a bride without spot or wrinkle. Will you be ready? It is here for you.

It is important to give the Lord glory, honour, and praise for who we are in Christ. There has been a process of incubation in my heart for a period of time by the Spirit of the Lord. The Lord can release supernatural rest upon us. I was born premature and underweight. This required that I be placed in an incubator for a period of time. There was a good chance that I wasn't going to survive. By the Lord's miracle-working power, I survived. Nobody would know I even had that experience. I grew from an underweight condition to a state of maturity where life became viable. This is what the Lord is doing; He is placing the church body into a position where life is not viable except through the power of the Holy Spirit. We need to purpose to achieve the objectives intended for our lives, objectives which He has determined before the foundation of the world.

The Lord desires for His signs, wonders, and miracles to return to their rightful place in the church. You are called to a mature life in the Spirit with Him. You no longer need an incubator. The Lord is creating you for the glory He may manifest in your life.

Have you ever watched someone make soup? Specific ingredients are put in at different stages. Some are added at the beginning of the process; once the water starts to boil, other ingredients are mixed in along the way. Everything boils together, and if you are successful you will take part in eating it, reaping the fruit of your labour.

God created us in His glory. We are a complete mixture of heavenly ingredients created in His image. Have you ever thought about it that way? I meditated on this for a while. Before the foundation of the world, the Lord created a recipe for you in His image and for His glory. You are made perfect in Him, and He sees you that way. When everything was perfect, He dispatched you into this world in His perfect timing. The glory is not for the sweet by and by. You are in the glory of God right now. It surrounds and envelops you. The thought of this gives me goose bumps. Understanding this aspect of His kingdom will change the way you look at life. Start praying for spiritual eyes to see who you really are in the glory of God. You are simply not an accident. This will allow you to look at life in a whole new way.

> And He raised us up together with Him and made us sit down together [giving us joint seating with Him] in the heavenly sphere [by virtue of our being] in Christ Jesus (the Messiah, the Anointed One). (Ephesians 2:6)

Created for First Class

You are first class. I say this because God is first class, and therefore so you are. Circumstances may tell you something else, but the Lord says you are first class. The Lord is heavenly, and so are you. Whether you believe this or not, the scripture states that we *"sit together in the heavenly places in Jesus Christ"* (Ephesians 2:6, NIV). Have you ever been on a plane and walked through first class, thinking, *Wow, it would be awesome to sit here?* You are meant for first class. You may not have the money to buy the ticket, but you are meant to sit in first class. Our God is first class, and He created you for first class.

A while ago, I travelled to Argentina for a wedding with Cathryn. My nephew, Pastor Chad McCabe, and his wonderful wife Daniella were getting married in Buenos Aires. While returning home to Canada, I prayed for an upgrade to first class seating (yes, you can ask for these things). I felt such an assurance that we were going to be upgraded. The length of the trip from Buenos Aires to Canada is twenty-three hours long. My wife and I arrived in Miami in the morning, where we had a six-hour layover. I suggested that we sit and relax in an airline lounge I had an access card to get into. Cathryn, Daniella, Chad, and I had all been travelling together, so we all went and sat in this lounge. There were only us and the lounge attendants there and the attendants outnumbered us two to one.

Suddenly, a tiny mouse scurried across the floor in front of our eyes. Cathryn and Daniella jumped up on two end tables and started screaming at the top of their lungs. Chad and I sat in our chairs, laughing hysterically at what was going on around us. The lounge attendants came running to find out what was going on; it was as if we were victims of a terrorist attack. We explained to the attendants exactly what had just happened. The senior attendant took it upon himself to bring us a bottle of wine as a result of the great trauma we had just experienced. We explained to him that we did not drink. Cathryn piped up and asked if we could be upgraded to first class for the rest of the flight home. That is exactly what happened.

Does God answer prayer in unusual ways? Does the Lord have a sense of humour? Absolutely! When you pray, the Lord hears you and answers, but you may not want to be my wife at that point in time. Wives, get ready to be used of God to answer your husband's prayers. It can work the other way around, too. This won't necessarily work every time, but the Lord hears your prayers. The glory of the Lord is on your life. It is your choice to believe this. You came from glory and you are going into glory. It is His desire to see His glory manifest in your life.

But we all, with unveiled face, beholding as in a mirror the glory of the Lord, are being transformed into the
same image from glory to glory, just as by the Spirit of
the Lord. (2 Corinthians 3:18, NKJV)

Three Phases of Glory

Great things are ahead for you and your family. There is destiny on
your life. We are on a "highway"—not a "low way." We need to refuse
the low way. We are on God's highway to glory. The Lord is releasing
the supernatural. You may be experiencing more visions and dreams
than usual. Do not underestimate what the Lord wants to download
to you in this season. The Lord asked me, "Do you want a piece of
me?" Not the whole pie, but He asked if I wanted a piece. It's time to
get ready for new revelation and understanding. People don't seem to
understand that we are not waiting for the glory; we are *"from glory to
glory."* Glory has three phases: we come from it, we are in it, and we are
going to it.

And out of the ground the Lord God made every tree
grow that is pleasant to the sight and good for food. The
tree of life was also in the midst of the garden, and the tree
of the knowledge of good and evil. (Genesis 2:9 NKJV)

Do not agree with any negative words that have been spoken over
your life. You are not an accident. You are here by divine appointment. There were two trees in the Garden—the Tree of Life and the
Tree of the Knowledge of Good and Evil. Draw from the Tree of Life.
The Tree of Life brings with it every attribute of the Lord, allowing

you to walk as He walked on this earth—in complete communion with the Father.

But now the righteousness of God has been revealed independently and altogether apart from the Law, although actually it is attested by the Law and the Prophets, namely, the righteousness of God which comes by believing with personal trust and confident reliance on Jesus Christ (the Messiah). [And it is meant] for all who believe. For there is no distinction, since all have sinned and are falling short of the honor and glory which God bestows and receives. [All] are justified and made upright and in right standing with God, freely and gratuitously by His grace (His unmerited favor and mercy), through the redemption which is [provided] in Christ Jesus, Whom God put forward [before the eyes of all] as a mercy seat and propitiation by His blood [the cleansing and life-giving sacrifice of atonement and reconciliation, to be received] through faith. This was to show God's righteousness, because in His divine forbearance He had passed over and ignored former sins without punishment. It was to demonstrate and prove at the present time (in the now season) that He Himself is righteous and that He justifies and accepts as righteous him who has [true] faith in Jesus. Then what becomes of [our] pride and [our] boasting? It is excluded (banished, ruled out entirely). On what principle? [On the principle] of doing good deeds? No, but on the principle of faith.

> For we hold that a man is justified and made upright
> by faith independent of and distinctly apart from good
> deeds (works of the Law). [The observance of the Law
> has nothing to do with justification.] (Romans 3:21–28)

This scripture is for you and me. You are made different because you are a son or daughter of the Most High. The Lord Jesus did this for us. Believers have the ability, therefore, to draw upon something that non-believers don't. You may have made mistakes in the past—one hundred percent of us have. There is no need to apologize for not being perfect; however, we must repent of sin when it enters our lives. In our own natural strength and ability, it is impossible to be perfect. You are completely incapable of perfection, and that is great. If we could do it, we would take the credit. The Lord did it.

Two thousand years ago, something took place that changed everything by the power of the cross. The only way to live in glory is through Him. The Old Testament is full of things you needed to achieve before you could enter the Holy of Holies. Much of religion tries to keep us in an unsanctified realm, but the reality is that you have been completely covered by the blood of the lamb. God did it all for us. If you are striving for something, stop! Receive it by faith. You are called to be Holy, blameless, and sinless by faith. Those who love the Lord will obey him. The issue is love. Do you love him?

> For it was in Him that all things were created, in heaven
> and on earth, things seen and things unseen, whether
> thrones, dominions, rulers, or authorities; all things
> were created and exist through Him [by His service,
> intervention] and in and for Him. (Colossians 1:16)

Restoration by the Lord

You were created in Christ and for Christ. Your mind may not be able to wrap itself around that. Why do people embark on home restoration projects? Because something breaks and needs restoration. Have you ever restored a home? God's into disaster restoration. He restores you and me. At one time, we were all disasters.

This past spring, our basement was flooded and it needed to be completely restored, which has become a long process. There was eight inches of water. Everything we had in our basement was virtually destroyed and needed to be replaced. You and I have been restored to a right relationship with the Lord through the finished work of the cross. It is a done deal. The Lord is the author of restoration, and not only to Him; it is also His desire to restore the relationships around you. To walk under an open heaven, you need to understand this principle. Your role is simply to accept it by faith and repent of sin when it enters your life.

Repentance releases an open heaven. The problem is that many people believe repentance means that we can go on sinning without consequence. Repentance actually means turning and moving in the complete opposite direction from where we were going. If we do that, He is faithful to forgive us. By the Spirit of the Lord, we go through inner restoration. I get excited about this. Once you catch the fullness of what the Lord has done, there will be a new kick to your step. Boldness for the Lord will flow through your life. Your authority is not dependent upon the world; it depends on Him. By the Spirit, you have nothing but Him, and when others see you they will see Christ; when you look in the mirror, you will see Him.

Each and every one of us has fallen short of the glory of God. He desires to release something that will restore what has been robbed from you and the glory of God in your life. When I look at a baby, I know that it came from heaven. It came from heaven on assignment to achieve something here on earth. It doesn't matter what you have believed in the past, or what negative words have been spoken over you. God is more than able to complete us. If you feel you are fully completed, I have news for you—you are not. If you stumble and fall, quickly get up and continue by the power of the Spirit of the Lord in your life.

> So then, whether you eat or drink, or whatever you may
> do, do all for the honor and glory of God. (1 Corinth-
> ians 10:31)

Have you ever gone to a pawn shop? If you have, it was probably because you needed money. In doing this, you took the "low way." That's what mankind did; they pawned off their birthright like Essau (Genesis 25:34). Do you know that the Lord loved Jacob but despised Essau, even before they were born? Even though Jacob was named the deceiver, why would God love him and despise Essau? I believe it was because Essau put no value on his heavenly birthright. Please, value your destiny! Value what the Lord has released for your life. Ensure that you guard and protect the Lord in your life. Instead of having glory, mankind went to a pawn shop and exchanged the glory of the Lord for something of lesser value—walking the earth with no value for the things of God. There must have been something desperate in humanity to make them go from up there to down here, where worldliness is more important than Godliness. The Lord has a "high way" for your life.

People need to make choices, even though the choices made may not always be right. The Lord chose us before we chose Him. God does not get in step with our lives; we need to get in step with His. A new pace is coming. You may not have always planned what has happened in your life nor received perhaps what you had desired out of life. You may not have thought you would end up where you are, but God knows what He is doing.

It is important to ask the Lord for supernatural revelation regarding who you are in His eyes. The enemy and the world will lie to you. The reality is that there is a realm of righteousness being released to you by His Holy Spirit. You are qualified in Him and called to make a difference. The difference you make is the fruit of a manifested heaven surrounding you. The mandate of heaven is upon you. You came from glory. You are in glory. You will go to glory.

CHAPTER FIVE

Heaven Knows Who You Are

The Devil is on the Run

I believe 2010 brought an explosion. The power of God wants to manifest in a way that has never been seen before. Christianity is not the same as it was. The bride is not the same as it was before. We have two choices—press forward into the realms the Lord is bringing us to, or sit back and watch the world pass us by.

It is time to press forward in the name of Jesus Christ. There is an amazing power of God being released. It is time to expect supernatural visits from the Lord consistently. A release is taking place. Getting into the presence of the Lord is much easier. The devil is on the run. I believe the Lord is saying, "The best defence is a strong offence." When the devil attacks, we need to become stronger in the Lord.

Seven years ago, I was massively attacked in my body one Saturday night. At that time, the church I pastor had prayer services on Saturday nights, so instead of going to prayer I drove to the hospital emergency room because of the intense pain I was experiencing in my body. It took until 4:00 a.m. for them to see me. They ran multiple tests on me for hours. After completing the tests, they couldn't find anything wrong.

I left around 8:00 a.m. Sunday morning. It took me fifteen minutes to drive from the hospital to my home. The whole way I said, "Devil, listen up! You will never attack me again in that area. I am going to preach the Gospel of the Lord with more fervency, zeal, and power of the Holy Spirit than ever before!" I have not been attacked in that area since.

The remedy to defeat is a strong offence. When the children of Israel saw giants in the land of promise, they wanted to turn around and run. That is not Christianity. Christianity is an offensive thrust into darkness. Darkness will try and attach itself to you. As a Christian, you need to shine the light that is in you. It is important as a believer to have a fervent zeal. No matter what happens, the kingdom of God is moving forward. You need to purpose to be a part of it. The devil can take his best shot, because he is already a defeated foe. We can't sit back as Christians and simply be spectators, which for the most part is the way Christianity has played out for millennia. We need to go in and occupy this land. It is not time to give ground. I want to agree with you, in name of Jesus Christ, that *"No weapon formed against you shall prosper"* (Isaiah 54:17, NKJV). The Lord sets the captives free and shakes every force of darkness. The devil is on the run; he just may not know it yet.

You Are Sent from Heaven

A few years ago, our family decided to go to the Fairmont Hot Springs in British Columbia, approximately four hundred miles from our home in Sylvan Lake, Alberta. My oldest son and daughter-in-law could not make it, but otherwise our complete family were there with us. One evening just before dusk, we all decided to take a walk to the hot springs, which is an incredibly beautiful natural setting in the mountains. To get to the hot spring, you walk down a gravelled walkway from the upper manmade pool to the springs.

Just as we arrived at the natural pool, two men came out of the hot pool as our family was about to enter. I engaged them in conversation. I observed two complete sets of dress suits on a rock within a meter or two of where we were standing, and of course I assumed these suits belonged to the men. It seemed odd to me to have two grown men go swimming in a hot pool after wearing suits.

Once my family had gone on ahead, one of them asked me, "Who are you?"

"My name is Peter Nash and I pastor a church in Sylvan Lake."

They replied, "We know who you are."

I will never forget those words. I didn't ask them, but I was thinking, *I wonder how they know who I am.*

My children were telling me to come into the pool and actually insisted on it. Before I went to join them, the two men said, "Bears come out on this path at night, so you might want to be careful and leave the area before then." I thanked them for the advice. I turned and took two steps towards the pool, looked back, and suddenly before my eyes the men were gone.

Two or three days later, I was thinking about my experience talking with these men. I thought to myself, *I wish I would have said more, or asked them a few more questions.* I believe this was a visitation from the angelic realm to purposely intervene in my life and the lives of those in my household. Do such visitations really occur? Absolutely, under a manifested heaven. In scripture, such visits are a regular reality. In fact, I believe the Lord has sovereignly intervened in my life to preserve me on no less than half a dozen occasions. These experiences are real and I believe that if you look back over your life with eyes to see, similar visitations may have occurred in your life as well. Get ready for such visitations to manifest in a greater way to establish His heavenly kingdom.

Heaven knows who you are. The scripture says, *"Just as He chose us in Him before the foundation of the world..."* (Ephesians 1:4, NKJV). This scripture says a lot to me. If you believe the Bible, you know that He knew you before you were in your mother's womb. He knows how many hairs are on your head. You are not an accident. There is supernatural mandate from heaven on your life. It is there. There is a realm of glory that defies all natural understanding. You are supernaturally empowered by the Spirit of the Lord. We have been sent here from heaven on assignment.

> Where could I go from Your Spirit? Or where could I flee from Your presence? (Psalms 139:7)

In this scripture, David is speaking. Things are going to start coming into your life in the near future that will defy all natural understanding. In the past, supernatural visitations have set fear into the church body. The Bible says we should not fear an angelic visitation (see Luke 1:13, 30). We have a tendency to fear the supernatural power of God. This fear has led to revivals shutting down. When the Lord God manifests, fear tries to creep in. The supernatural realm transcends our minds. The mind of Christ is available to us to help us see these manifestations by the Spirit of the Lord.

When we press into more of His presence, the Spirit of the Lord is revealed. Rather than shutting it down, we need to go deeper into the things of God. When the Spirit is revealed, it will always line up with the things of God and His Word. It will not deceive you. It will take you deeper into the realm of God's glory.

I am a very logical and analytical person, but the Lord has never worked logically in my life. I have had miracle after miracle happen, actual lifesaving occurrences that defy all of my natural mindsets. They never come the way I think they will. Why do we let these things bog us down? In the Bible, Naaman had to dip in the River Jordan seven times. He couldn't understand why he couldn't wash himself in his own country waters (see 2 Kings 5:10–12). That wasn't the Lord's plan. The Lord's will always defies our natural thinking. Have you ever had a miracle of God happen the way you thought it would?

> O Lord, you have searched me [thoroughly] and have known me. You know my downsitting and my uprising; You understand my thought afar off. You sift and search out my path and my lying down, and You are acquainted with all my ways. For there is not a word in my tongue [still unuttered], but, behold, O Lord, You know it altogether. You have beset me and shut me in—behind and before, and You have laid Your hand upon me. Your [infinite] knowledge is too wonderful for me; it is

high above me, I cannot reach it. Where could I go from Your Spirit? Or where could I flee from Your presence? (Psalms 139:1–7)

The Lord knows who you are. His wisdom, knowledge, and understanding transcend your thinking. There are many things in the natural that we can think and talk about, but God's thoughts are way above our thoughts. God knows more than we will ever know—even about things we think we understand. The presence of God changes everything. That is why we need to seek His presence in our lives.

It's Time to Carry the Lord

Search me [thoroughly], O God, and know my heart! Try me and know my thoughts! And see if there is any wicked or hurtful way in me, and lead me in the way everlasting. (Psalms 139:23–24)

At the church I pastor, we have early morning prayer. One Friday morning, I had a visitation from the Lord. He brought me to a piggy-back race. I was able to carry the Lord. I could feel His weight on my back, and I said, "Get off!" I realized quickly what I had done. I immediately repented, saying, "Lord. forgive me. I am so sorry!"

I want the Lord on my back. Many of us are carrying things on our back all the time. We need to be carrying the Lord Jesus Christ on our backs—not the cares and concerns of our lives. At times we don't want to carry Him, and that is why I repented. It is time to realize that carrying the Lord is a lot better than the things we carry. Why refuse to carry the Lord? This should be the only thing we want to carry.

It is a new day. We need to carry the Lord in our lives and hearts like never before. This is the Lord's desire. Things look hard sometimes, but as we pick up our stride it becomes easier. I feel the Lord is calling us to do this. The scripture says, *"For my yoke is easy and my burden is light"* (Matthew 11:30, NKJV). The Lord is speaking. He rebuked me when I thought His burden was heavy. He said, "My burden is light!" You can receive or reject this is in your heart. I know I am going to a different realm. I am refusing the things that deny the power of God in my life. I challenge you to do the same.

> For He shall give His angels charge over you, to keep you
> in all your ways. (Psalms 91:11, NKJV)

His burden is light and will release the grace and mercy of the power of God. Then you will be able to achieve all He has for you. The Lord's angels will charge over you when you are obedient to Him. It is time to achieve a new level of obedience. It comes with a cost. You need to lay down your burdens and pick up the cross.

CHAPTER SIX

Moving Locations

Changing Your Spiritual Position

In life, people resist change. We like staying in the same place, entrenched in the status quo. As I write this, I am on a plane flying over the Pacific Ocean from Southeast Asia returning from a ministry trip. While headed to the airport this morning, I sensed the Lord saying to me that fear is a powerful force and that most of Christianity would not die for the sake of the Gospel, nor go to where the Lord would ask them to go. I began to weep in the taxi, knowing full well that it was fear that prevented sincere believers from walking under a manifested heaven.

It is fear that keeps many from obedience to Christ. He may not ask you to become a martyr, but you need to be obedient in whatever He asks. The only way to know if it is Him or not is to continually examine your own heart. When you walk into church on Sunday morning, most of the time people sit roughly in the same place. If someone moved to a completely new place, you may think, *I wonder why he moved.* Different reasons for the move might pop up in your head. If someone was in the spot you usually sit in, you may think, *Hey, what is happening?*

There are so many thoughts competing for our mind's attention that are not of God. You need to be able to change your position for the end times and take captive every thought that exalts itself against the knowledge of God. The change needs to be in your spiritual positioning. It is time to position yourself where God is, far above principalities, powers, and rulers of darkness in high places. Don't focus on garbage. Focus on getting into the position the Lord has called you to be in under a manifested heaven.

Shake yourself up. You don't need anyone to shake you. Life is not all about fun and games. Everything that can be shaken will be shaken in order that what remains be completely in Him. Religion tries to enter in and say, "It's okay. We can come to church and feel really good about ourselves." But there is a higher realm we need to go to.

The Lord has been dealing with brokenness in my life. He said, "Peter, you're not broken enough. Your heart is not contrite enough." It's time to get out of your mind and get into His. *"We are more than conquerors through Him who loved us"* (Romans 8:37, NKJV). Those are not just nice, fancy words you read on a page. It's time to get over your problems and realize you are positioned on the other side. This doesn't mean you won't get attacked; after all, Christ was crucified. When you do things for God, all hell will come against it.

There are two things that I want to focus on in this chapter.

1. Where are you now?

2. If you're not seated above principalities, powers, and rulers of darkness, how do you get to where God wants you to be?

Obstacles will keep coming into your life, trying to get you away from your position with the Lord Jesus Christ. You need to realize that you are positioned far above principalities, powers, and rulers of darkness. He has *"raised us up together, and made us sit together in the heavenly places in Christ Jesus"* (Ephesians 2:6, NKJV). I grieve for people who cannot understand this. If you are attacked by finances, relationships, or sin, you will continue to go around and around until understanding hits that area. You can only get it right with the Lord's help. Everybody is dysfunctional. We need to learn from what we've been through, unless you want to keep heading around the same mountain, saying, "Poor me."

The Lord has blessed me with the gifting of mercy. Mercy is better than judgment. The Lord has made a way for us to walk above all our circumstances out of His mercy. He has given us the tools and weapons we need to achieve everything He desires for us. Not everyone will be in the same position.

It's time to change your spiritual position. God is making a way. Do not predetermine where you are spiritually. I would guarantee it is too low. God will exceed your expectation. We need to expand our ideas and see by the Spirit of the Lord. He already has your seat predetermined. We can't see it with our natural minds. The reality is that most Christians don't accept the position that has been set aside for them.

God's Way, Not Your Way

The key is to be obedient to what God is asking. I do not counsel people as often as I used to, and in many ways there is a natural resistance to doing things the way the Lord has intended. How many times can you tell someone the same thing? If people do not want to be obedient or accept the advice that I give, should I keep saying the same thing?

I once had a couple come to me for counselling. The first week, it took me over two hours to get to the point. One of the spouses would not forgive the other spouse. I have found that forgiveness is an incredible key in unlocking a manifested heaven in and around your life. The next week, the same issue kept coming up. Essentially, we had to go over the same territory that we had walked through one week earlier. We had to take the ground and release forgiveness again. When I met with the couple the next week, the same topic came up again. I said, "Listen! Enough is enough. I cannot counsel you anymore. If you can't take the steps we have already covered, I can't keep saying the same thing."

In the Bible it says,

> Then Peter came to Him and said, "Lord, how often shall my brother sin against me, and I forgive him? Up to seven times?"
>
> Jesus said to him, "I do not say to you, up to seven times, but up to seventy times seven." (Matthew 18:21–22, NKJV).

I know that I have to forgive *"seventy times seven,"* but there has to be a point where you stop saying the same thing over and over. Why not get it right the first time? We have to get the revelation from Him.

We have to walk it out biblically and see what the Bible says about the issue. Many times, people want their way—not God's way—unless, of course, they actually become the same under a surrendered lifestyle and a manifested heaven.

You're the Biggest Obstacle

Your position on earth directly links to your seat in the heavenly realm. If you don't see yourself there, you are not "under" the things God has promised for your life. That is not Christianity. If you don't want more of the Lord, you should join the rotary club or the local legion.

Hunger and thirst are keys to seeing the kingdom of heaven advance. There are places where people get together and never mention Jesus or the ability He has given us. Fellowship is great and incredibly important for any vibrant and functioning church, but it is not the most important part of the experience. The presence of the Lord is the most important key to experiencing a manifested heaven in your life. You won't mention how you are more than a conqueror in Christ at a rotary club meeting. However, you will have fun and go home feeling really good about yourself. That is religion, by the way. Religion is having a form of godliness but denying the power of God to change and transform.

Don't get me wrong, I am all for social interaction, but the presence of God desires to change your life. You may feel pretty good where you are at. I say, "No, you need to change." You need to get over yourself. The biggest obstacle in your life is not the devil. It is you. I know this because I am the biggest obstacle to heaven manifesting in my life.

One day in morning prayer, I was meditating on an upcoming counselling session I would be having. The person had drug and alcohol problems. In my own mind, I was becoming a little self-righteous and the Lord gave me a scripture out of the blue, and a strategy to deal with that situation. It was a scripture I would never have thought of, but it was more applicable for me than the person I was going to counsel. The scripture goes like this: *"Hypocrite! First remove the plank from your own eye, and then you will see clearly to remove the speck from your brother's eye"* (Matthew 7:5, NKJV).

Life experience develops the way we look at life. We have all had our own experiences. This plays a big part in the way we react to things. I come from a police background. Police, for the most part, look at everyone as "guilty until proven innocent." I had to repent from that mindset before I could be an effective minister. Can the Lord change your mindsets? Not only does He want to, but He will, if you give Him the opportunity. It's okay to repent and get back on track.

I have heard it said that when you are steering a big oceanliner, being off by a degree can change your destination by hundreds of miles. We want to be bang on with the Lord, and we do not want to miss anything He desires for us. I was able to remove the "speck" from my brother's eye only once I dealt with the "plank" from my own eye. It is easy for us to see the plank in someone else's eye, but it may be a speck in comparison to what may be in our own eye. I thank God that I was given the gift of mercy. I simply need to apply it in every situation and circumstance. In the Lord's view, mercy is infinitely better than judgement.

The Lord Qualifies Us

If you see yourself as more than a conqueror, that's exactly what you are. It's always a matter of positioning by the Spirit of the Lord. My wife Cathryn, who is amazing and has a lot of wisdom, often says, "Will the rock fall on you or will you fall on the rock of Jesus Christ?" In my own strength, I am incapable. There is one who did it for us—the Lord Jesus Christ. This qualifies us and makes us capable. The Lord keeps saying to me, "Continually be broken. Not in a negative way, but be broken and contrite." Many resist this thought. Many want to make themselves, but it is only in the strength of the Lord that we can enter into the heavenly realm. It has never been about what we can achieve but about what *He* has achieved.

Jesus was opposed because He challenged religious thinking on every level, including this level. I want nothing of myself to remain. I want more of Him. The way to get there is through brokenness and surrender. It has to become a lifestyle. It doesn't matter if people have hurt or wounded you. It says in the Bible, *"Love your enemies"* (Luke 6:27, NKJV). I say, "The greater the incision, the greater the healing." Life is about perspective, so let it be His perspective for your life.

You Are Seated in the Heavenly Realm

> By having the eyes of your heart flooded with light, so that you can know and understand the hope to which He has called you, and how rich is His glorious inheritance in the saints (His set-apart ones), and [so that you can know and understand] what is the immeasurable and unlimited and surpassing greatness of His power in and for us who believe, as demonstrated in the working of His mighty strength, which He exerted in Christ when He raised Him from the dead and seated Him at His [own] right hand in the heavenly [places]. (Ephesians 1:18–20)

Where are you seated today? This is a question only you can answer. Are you above or below the spiritual position the Lord has for you at this point in your life? You may not have your heart flooded with light yet, but do not feel bad about this. We are rich in his glorious inheritance. Rich! The scripture says that God *"raised Him from the dead and seated Him at His [own] right hand in the heavenly [places]."* He is seated in the heavenly realms.

> And He raised us up together with Him and made us sit down together [giving us joint seating with Him] in the heavenly sphere [by virtue of our being] in Christ Jesus (the Messiah, the Anointed One). (Ephesians 2:6)

This scripture applies to you—*"He raised us up together with Him."* He seated us together in *"the heavenly sphere."* Do you believe the Bible? This is for all of us. Yes, even for your neighbour or the guy down the street, but more importantly it is for you.

Seek Eternal Treasures

> If then you have been raised with Christ [to a new life, thus sharing His resurrection from the dead], aim at and seek the [rich, eternal treasures] that are above, where Christ is, seated at the right hand of God. (Colossians 3:1)

It is time to seek eternal treasures. Worldly treasures do not matter. You need to get the full revelation of where you are positioned in heaven. *"Your kingdom come, Your will be done on earth as it is in heaven"* (Matthew 6:10, NKJV). Heaven is available on earth. You don't want to go around the same mountain over and over again. You are seated far above principalities, powers, and rulers of darkness. Rise above!

It's Time to Get Hungry

> For you say, I am rich; I have prospered and grown wealthy, and I am in need of nothing; and you do not realize and understand that you are wretched, pitiable, poor, blind, and naked. (Revelation 3:17)

Most North Americans have the mentality that they have no needs. They are most certainly not looking for God. I was recently in Africa and continue to travel there regularly. I had the opportunity there to attend a church with a tin roof. They had lawn chairs for seats. When I was there, I sowed $100 U.S. dollars. After service, I went to the pastor's house for lunch. I can't remember if we had chicken or goat. What I do remember is that they ate every part of it. They did not waste one part of the animal. This showed me that they are hungry people. In North America, we spit stuff out because we are not hungry enough. In Africa, they eat everything to satisfy their hunger—including eating bark off trees simply to stay alive. Centuries ago, Native Americans would carefully stalk the much-prized buffalo. Once killed, they would utilize every ounce of it to stay alive. They did this because they were hungry. They did this because they were unsure of when or where the next meal would come from.

There is a great lack of hunger and thirst in North America for the things of God. People are satisfied where they are at. They say, "Pastor, don't rock the boat. I am comfortable with my life." The Lord is saying, "This is coming to an end." The Bible says, "*Whoever tries to preserve his life will lose it, but whoever loses his life will preserve and quicken it"* (Luke 17:33). If you lose everything, you will gain through this loss—but don't do it for the gain. People are living for the now, not for eternity. In the end, this will not work. It is time for the comfortable people of this world to be shaken. There is a new realm coming, if you allow it. You need to be desperate for more of the Lord and desperate for His mighty move on the earth.

CHAPTER SEVEN

One Thing

One thing should occupy our focus—the mandate of heaven. Issues should not be the focus, because the mandate of heaven is upon us. Do not allow issues to rule your life. Heaven has been released by God for your life. This is all that our lives should be about. Our carnal nature doesn't want to serve God. Struggling and wrestling goes on within us. The grace and mercy of the Lord needs to be released into our lives. A heavenly assignment has been placed on every person. The assignment is more than just getting through things the world throws at us. I am more after the spiritual than the natural.

Go After the Higher Life

> Whoever finds his [lower] life will lose it [the higher
> life], and whoever loses his [lower] life on My account
> will find it [the higher life]. (Matthew 10:39)

There are good things in the world that are not God-things. We need to find our "lower life" so that we can lose it. In the Garden there were two trees—the Tree of Life and the Tree of the Knowledge of Good and Evil. One tree was good and the other was bad. This shows that from the beginning of time there was good and bad available.

There are efforts brought forth by man to create order in the world. These efforts will not work. Safety cannot be created by mankind, but we often see these efforts made. The sole purpose of this movement is to bring the antichrist. Man's way of safety and security is the "lower life." There is an abundance of things in the world created to bring comfort. A few examples would be lights and automatic car starters; I don't necessarily believe that these things are from the Lord.

We need to be after the "higher life," the spiritual life. Enoch walked with God and *"was caught up and transferred to heaven"* (Hebrews 11:5). He was taken. Christianity may not believe this, but it could happen again. The scripture says, *"For there is no respect of persons with God"* (Romans 2:11, NKJV). I want to get out of my natural mind and adopt the mind of Christ. There is only one person who is normal—the Lord Jesus Christ. He is the only one we should be after. He is the only one who makes a difference in our lives.

Become Deeply Intimate with the Lord

I represent the Open Bible Faith Fellowship (OBFF). I am one of its directors. The leader is Rick Ciaramitaro. One time, I was driving with Rick to a board meeting in Kitchener, Ontario. We were fifteen minutes late. He said to me, "Any second now, my wife will be calling. She'll want to know why we are late." Literally five seconds later, it happened. He looked over at me and said, "I told you so." The reality is that they are intimate with each other. They know exactly what each other will do and when. This applies to the relationship we need to desire with the Lord. We need to be so intimate with Him that we know His thoughts, heart, and can predict what He wants us to do. It is impossible to attract people without this kind of relationship. We need the mind of Christ to know what the Lord desires for our lives.

> But whatever former things I had that might have been gains to me, I have come to consider as [one combined] loss for Christ's sake. Yes, furthermore, I count everything as loss compared to the possession of the priceless privilege (the overwhelming preciousness, the surpassing worth, and supreme advantage) of knowing Christ Jesus my Lord and of progressively becoming more deeply and intimately acquainted with Him [of perceiving and recognizing and understanding Him more fully and clearly]. For His sake I have lost everything and consider it all to be mere rubbish (refuse, dregs), in order that I may win (gain) Christ (the Anointed One), and that I may [actually] be found and known as in Him, not having any [self-achieved] righteousness that

can be called my own, based on my obedience to the
Law's demands (ritualistic uprightness and supposed
right standing with God thus acquired), but possessing
that [genuine righteousness] which comes through faith
in Christ (the Anointed One), the [truly] right standing
with God, which comes from God by [saving] faith. [For
my determined purpose is] that I may know Him [that
I may progressively become more deeply and intimately
acquainted with Him, perceiving and recognizing and
understanding the wonders of His Person more strongly
and more clearly], and that I may in that same way come
to know the power outflowing from His resurrection
[which it exerts over believers], and that I may so share
His sufferings as to be continually transformed [in spirit
into His likeness even] to His death, [in the hope] that if
possible I may attain to the [spiritual and moral] resurrection [that lifts me] out from among the dead [even
while in the body]. Not that I have now attained [this
ideal], or have already been made perfect, but I press on
to lay hold of (grasp) and make my own, that for which
Christ Jesus (the Messiah) has laid hold of me and made
me His own. I do not consider, brethren, that I have captured and made it my own [yet]; but one thing I do [it
is my one aspiration]: forgetting what lies behind and
straining forward to what lies ahead, I press on toward
the goal to win the [supreme and heavenly] prize to
which God in Christ Jesus is calling us upward. So let
those [of us] who are spiritually mature and full-grown

have this mind and hold these convictions; and if in any respect you have a different attitude of mind, God will make that clear to you also. (Philippians 3:7–15)

Paul is speaking about his former life in this scripture. He was an elite trained and educated Pharisee. For a season of time, he killed Christians.

I am after total and complete intimacy with Christ. I want His mind and nothing else. This should be the mandate that we are after in the body of Christ. *"I count everything as loss compared to the possession of the priceless privilege of knowing Christ Jesus my Lord."* The word "knowing" is really about being consumed with Christ. Just knowing about Christ doesn't cut it.

Neville Johnson stated a great reality in one of his messages. In a paraphrased form, he said that the Christian church has the Bible, but the people who actually walked with the Lord had no written instruction. You can know every scripture and still have no relationship with the Lord. You can attend church and feel great about yourself. I go to church to get more of the Lord Jesus Christ. He needs to be the operator of our lives. We need to progressively become *"more deeply and intimately acquainted with Him."*

It's Time to Go Up

Everything in this world that is not of the Lord is mere rubbish. We need to be completely free of all righteousness that can be called our own. Self-righteousness is so ungodly. You do not have the right to look down on others because they do not measure up to your righteousness. Christianity puts people in the Bible like Paul on a pedestal.

We somehow believe that we can't be like them. The reality is that we can. The Lord has created us this way. It is time to get out of your mindsets so that you can see and perceive like God. This needs to be our determined purpose. Is it wrong to want to become more *"deeply and intimately acquainted with Him"*? Some Christians think so. They believe that they are happy with their lives. *"For as [a man] thinks in his heart, so is he"* (Proverbs 23:7, NKJV).

There are "wonders" of the Lord Jesus Christ. The Lord wants to reveal secrets and mysteries to you. God chose you before you chose Him. We can be like Paul. Ultimately, I want to be like Jesus. The only way to achieve this is to press on. We need to be *"forgetting what lies behind and straining forward to what lies ahead."* Straining comes with resistance. The Lord is calling us upward. Your focus needs to be up, not down or sideways, but upward. You need to become spiritually mature and full grown. Everyone is at a different level of spiritual maturity. That is not bad. Press on at whatever level you are at, so that you may go upwards. This is the Word of God. We need to plant it deep in our hearts—not by our own strength, but in the Lord. The only qualification you need is hunger and thirst. Allow the Holy Spirit to work in your life.

CHAPTER EIGHT

Preparation Time Is Coming to an End

In times of revival, the enemy will try to rob communication. The enemy desires to disrupt what God wants to do. Opposition to the kingdom only means one thing—you are headed in the right direction. The devil is opposed to you. He is opposed to the kingdom of God advancing in and around your life. Have you ever done something knowing you heard from the Lord and someone tries to stop you? Every assignment taken on from the kingdom of God will be opposed by the enemy, but you must ensure that you are hearing clearly by the Spirit of the Lord.

At the beginning of 2010, the Lord told me that I had been ordained for 2010 and that 2010 had been ordained for me. When you receive something from the Lord, all hell comes against it. Remember that Jesus was opposed, the apostles were opposed, and the kingdom is opposed. Jesus had many disciples leave Him. People lied about Him. People twisted His words to get Him off-guard. They wanted Him to come down from a position of authority to a lower realm. They wanted Him to come from a position of being above realms of darkness to below them. Always go up, never come down.

God is doing tremendous things. *"For the children of Israel walked forty years in the wilderness…"* (Joshua 5:6, NKJV). It is time to go forward and walk through the River Jordan into your promised land. We do not to go back to the wilderness. This is dependent on the positioning of the Lord in your life. The Lord has given you and me authority in the spiritual realm. We can believe it because it says in the Bible, *"Behold, I give you the authority to trample on serpents and scorpions, and over all the power of the enemy, and nothing shall by any means hurt you"* (Luke 10:19, NKJV).

Christianity is not about how capable you are in walking out your life here on earth; it is all about walking out your life here on earth, empowered and infused by His ability in you. I believe in the government of God. I didn't choose to be in full-time ministry; He chose me. He chose us on purpose, *"before the foundation of the world"* (Ephesians 1:4, NKJV). Only He can fulfill your destiny. If that doesn't blow your mind, I don't know what will. Your abilities don't matter. If you think you have an ability, lay it down or it will be taken. Moses knew he was incapable in himself. The less ability and strength you have the better. *"But God has chosen the foolish things of the world to put to shame the wise, and God has chosen the weak things of the world to put to shame the things which are mighty"* (1 Corinthians 1:27, NKJV).

People Need the Lord Jesus Christ

God is using the complete church to achieve His objectives, plans, and purposes. This is the time and hour to get what the Lord desires for you in the throne room, which you can approach through His grace. The equipping that you need is available. You are not on earth by coincidence or accident. I do not believe in coincidences; I believe in divine appointments.

One time another driver backed into my vehicle. The guy got out and started to yell and scream. I was not concerned about this, because of my background. I got him in the back of my vehicle. He was still swearing and cursing at me. I said to him, "I am a pastor retired from the RCMP." Suddenly, everything changed. I shared the Gospel with him. When he left, he said to me, "I am so sorry for swearing." Ninety five percent of the people I meet are easy to love. Many people make me want to cry just by seeing what they have had to walk through in their lives. I know that they need the Lord Jesus Christ and feel they have nobody to turn to. There is a way, and it is in the grace of the Lord. Like Paul, we can say, *"[His] grace is sufficient for [me]."*

In my career as an RCMP officer, I was once a watch commander. A watch commander runs the detachment and supervises all officers on the street. On one occasion, a lady phoned in. She was in tears speaking with our dispatcher. She explained that her husband had consumed eighteen beers and was driving around with a driving prohibition. He had his three children with him. The children were all under six years of age. I placed three police cars out in the area to look for him. About an hour later, she called in again. She wanted to follow up on our progress in finding her husband and children. I said to her, "No, we haven't found them yet." I told her that I would go out myself and try and find him.

This wasn't part of my job. I took a long drive away from our detachment headquarters and found the husband and children.

In the RCMP, I tried to refrain from using handcuffs unless there was a need to do so. I felt the Lord wanted that. I practice this as a pastor, too, and I never want to spiritually handcuff people. I arrested that gentleman and placed him in the back of the police car. I had a female constable escort the children back to the mother. This guy had cowboy boots on. He started to kick the back window of the police car, and I casually said to him, "Please stop doing that, or I will have to handcuff you." He responded with comments such as, "I am going to kick the [bleep] out of you" and "I am going to kill you."

I laughed, got out the car, and opened the back door. I started to pull him out. In the process, he planted his feet under the shelf in the back of the car. My first attempted failed. At that point, I lost it. Even a pastor can admit when he loses it. I pulled him out of the car and placed him in handcuffs. Through this process, I managed to pull all of the tendons in my pinkie finger. I still have a crooked pinkie to remind me. I saw a plastic surgeon to repair the tendons the next day.

Two days later, this gentleman was still sitting in the police cells. In my normal clothes, I went down to see him. I had a sling around my arm. The first thing he said to me was, "What in the world happened to you?"

"Don't you remember?" I asked. Then I told him the story.

What happened next shocked me. He broke down in tears and said, "I never intended for anybody to get hurt."

To this day, those words resonate in my heart. The reality is that people don't know how to deal with the issues of life. This gentleman probably had a fight with his wife. In his mind, he thought, *I will take the three kids and drive around. This will scare the wits out of her.*

There are multitudes of people out there like this individual. Like all of us, many times throughout our lives it is difficult to deal with the issues of life without the Lord Jesus Christ. There is a better way for you and me, and it is under the redemptive blood of the lamb. People at times have a hard time dealing with the issues life throws at them. The only solution is Jesus Christ, our Lord and Saviour. He is the only way to have heaven manifest in your life.

The Lord Uses Dreams and Visions

I have noticed there is a real interest in society about things that can't be explained. For the most part, people do not realize that dreams and visions consume one-third of the Bible. I have received many dreams and visions from the Lord. I hope for more. It is important to understand that not all dreams and visions come from God, though. The movie *Inception* describes four-layer dreams. Paul Keith Davis, of White Dove Ministries, once shared with me that he entered into a three-layer dream. I am lucky if I get one! The Lord uses dreams and visions. *"After these things the word of the Lord came to Abram in a vision, saying, 'Do not be afraid, Abram. I am your shield, your exceedingly great reward'"* (Genesis 15:1, NKJV).

Doing things for the Lord can come at the most inopportune times. For example, the weekend our family was called to go to Bible school, Cathryn's dad found out he was having an operation. The doctor informed him and the family that he wouldn't make it through the weekend. That Monday, we left for Bible school and came back over a year later. We were still visiting with Cathryn's dad when we got home. It would have seemed like the most inopportune time to head off to Bible school. I say, "Don't go when things look easy; go when things look hard and you know you have clearly heard from the Lord in your course of action."

When people tell me that they are want to start coming to the church I pastor, I don't make it easy for them. I don't paint an unrealistic picture of church life. I usually say to them, "We have spiritual warfare, you will be opposed, and the enemy will try and take you out." I do this for a specific reason. I want people to come and be planted for the right reasons, not the wrong reasons. People must be planted to flourish with the Lord and not come for any other reason but the Lord.

> And go quickly and tell His disciples that He is risen from the dead, and indeed He is going before you into Galilee; there you will see Him. Behold, I have told you. (Matthew 28:7, NKJV)

The Lord gave me this scripture after one of our annual camp meetings on August 23, 2009, during our daily morning prayer services. I love to listen to what the Lord is saying to me. He illuminated this scripture to me and said, "You need to go to Galilee. I will reveal myself to you there." I received this word in my heart and said, "No matter what, I will get there." Of course, all hell broke loose. This happens when I hear from the Lord. It is important not to let your life be dictated by circumstances. No matter what people say, do what the Lord tells you. You need the revelation that God works through dreams and visions. Sure enough, in late November of that year I was sitting on the Sea of Galilee and received a supernatural visitation of the Lord Jesus.

The Lord Is Changing His Disciples' Garments

That November, I was in Israel with my fellow pastor and good friend Moses. We had been going to every border and praying for Israel and that His plans and purposes be fulfilled for His nation. On November 28, 2009, I found myself in a *kibbutz* on the south end of the Sea of Galilee. I was waiting on the balcony for Moses' and my wife to pack their bags.

That's when the word from the Lord came back to me and I entered into a vision. I saw the Lord cloaked in fine white linen, walking on the water. He was heading towards His disciples. They were in a boat. The disciples were wearing multi-colour garments. As Jesus got into the boat, all of the disciples' garments turned white. They matched Jesus perfectly.

A disciple is someone who believes in Him. This vision meant that He is changing His disciples' garments and that they will match Him perfectly. They are no longer multi-coloured; they are white as He is white. The Lord is coming for a bride without spot or wrinkle. I thanked the Lord for this vision, because it is not up to me to make these things happen; He is the one to do it. When testing and trials of ministry come, I do not have to be concerned because it is Him who is perfecting the bride—not me. If I hadn't been obedient and gone to Israel, I wouldn't have received this vision from the Lord.

Revelation releases something into the spiritual atmosphere that defies all natural understanding. Many times, we try to wrap our minds around what the Lord is doing and we cannot, because our minds have been conditioned for an earthly experience, not a heavenly experience. Oh, that we would have eyes to see by the Spirit that is resident in our lives. I stand on the Word that His church will become the bride. Not everyone in the church will be the bride, but if you allow Him in you will be a part of it. What exciting times we live in!

Something is released through revelation. I believe in the concept of the weed and tares growing up together. It says in the Bible, *"But while men slept, his enemy came and sowed tares among the wheat and went his way"* (Matthew 13:25, NKJV). The tares were not plucked out and thrown in the fire until the end of the age. The reality is that not everyone is a weed, nor is everyone wheat. All issues in life flow out of the heart. It is not about what people do or say. What matters is what you do when they attack your heart, reacting in a Godly way. When you are under persecution and attack, don't rise up and get angry. The key is to continue in love towards every person. If love is your foundation, heaven will manifest in your life. Remember what it says in Galatians 2:20—*"I am crucified with Christ: nevertheless I live; yet not I, but Christ liveth in me"* (KJV). What a principle to walk by.

> Another of the disciples said to Him, Lord, let me first go and bury [care for till death] my father. But Jesus said to him, Follow Me, and leave the dead [in sin] to bury their own dead. And after He got into the boat, His disciples followed Him. And suddenly, behold, there arose a violent storm on the sea, so that the boat was being covered up by the waves; but He was sleeping. And they went and awakened Him, saying, Lord, rescue and preserve us! We are perishing! And He said to them, Why are you timid and afraid, O you of little faith? Then He got up and rebuked the winds and the sea, and there was a great and wonderful calm (a perfect peaceableness). (Matthew 8:21–26)

The disciple said to Jesus, *"Lord, let me first go and bury [care for till death] my father."* This happened right before Jesus walked on the Sea of Galilee. The disciple wanted to go and bury his father. You can think you are alive and breathing but be dead in the Lord. Not everyone who walks into church is a Christian, and of course the Lord can change that in an instant of time. People need to awake to the realities of God.

When the disciples were following the will of God, a storm came up. This happens time and time again to put us in fear in our lives. Jesus was sleeping. The disciples were shocked that Jesus stayed sleeping through the storm. Jesus may have been exhausted, but He also knew the Father's will and that dying this way was not part of the plan. He knew the storm and what was going on and had no need to panic. He said to the disciples, *"O you of little faith."* In my eyes, faith means spiritually revealed truth. You may have a different way of defining faith, but this is what I believe the Lord has given me as a definition. Jesus then *"rebuked the winds and the sea, and there was a great and wonderful calm."* All hell will come against you when you follow the will of God. Remember in these times to have faith and see things as He sees them. I believe storms help us to be on our face before our Lord. We must totally and completely believe that He who has started a good work in us stands ready to complete it. Heaven on earth is all about the completion of our lives in Him to touch this world.

The Tabernacle in the Wilderness

The Lord gave me another vision on December 18, 2009, which I briefly mentioned in an earlier chapter. I was in morning prayer when I entered into this vision. In this vision I found myself in Moses' tabernacle, the tabernacle in the wilderness as Israel journeyed from Egypt to the Promised Land. This is significant because I also believe that a manifested heaven is in your promised land. I found myself in the outer court of the temple area. It was nice there. The presence of God was around, but I couldn't go in any further. I could definitely sense the Lord in this outer court experience.

Most of Christianity is in the outer court. They continue to be dictated to by their circumstances and plagued by issues and problems. In the Bible, the apostles were not swayed by finding themselves in jail, in chains, persecuted, or stoned. They didn't stay under these circumstances nor did circumstances cause them to stop proclaiming the advancing kingdom of heaven on this earth. They rose up, empowered by the Holy Spirit. The Lord *"raised us up together, and made us sit together in the heavenly places in Christ Jesus"* (Ephesians 2:6, NKJV). People stay *under* when the Lord has called us *over* the things that come against our lives.

It is the enemy's desire to keep us in a low place. At Pentecost, there was a release of the Holy Spirit. Peter denied the Lord three times. When empowered by the Holy Spirit, he became the boldest most, powerful man of God after Christ. When the Holy Spirit moves, boldness comes over us. This is available to you. You need to have the revelation that you are an overcomer. The Bible says, *"When I am weak, then I am strong"* (2 Corinthians 12:10, NKJV). We may be weak, but He is strong. I try to be weak so that He can be strong in my life. If you are walking around the mountain, I say, "Get your focus on the Lord. Get it back on Him."

In the vision, I was in the outer court having a great time. All of a sudden, I noticed the Lord Jesus at the door of the Holy of Holies. He said to me, "Come over here, I want to give you something." Being the obedient type, I walked right over. We entered into the inner court. In front of me was the Ark of the Covenant. The lid was off and I could see it in one corner with the cherubs at each end facing inward. The Lord then said to me, "Look inside the Ark of the Covenant. Here are the gifts I want to give you." I looked inside and there were three things.

To that point in time, I had been saved for over thirty-five years. To God, a day is like a thousand years and a thousand years is like a day. The Lord gave me access to the Holy of Holy's the day I was saved, not on the day I first saw it in this vision. It took me thirty-five years to see it in the Spirit. You may be thinking, *He's a slow learner*—which is a correct assumption. That's totally okay by me, because we all need to be led by revelation, not the letter of the Law. I am just happy the Lord showed this to me.

Immediately I repented to the Lord and said, "Should I have seen this thirty-five years ago?"

"You were made for such a time as this," the Lord replied.

The reason I bring this up is because you may feel you are not where you should be. If you allow the Lord to work, He will bring you to the place He desires for you. This is why it is so important not to ever give up on anybody, including yourself. Walking in the realm of the Spirit under a manifested heaven cannot be achieved in your own strength; the Lord is the one who does the work. Do not beat yourself up. We have only touched the tip of the iceberg in terms of revelation from the Lord, but revelation of Christ empowers you to walk in the heavenly realm here on earth. In the end of the age, which I believe is now upon us, the mysteries and secrets will be revealed. Those things that have been hidden down through the ages will be revealed under a manifested heaven. It is going to happen in an accelerated way and I totally believe it is upon us in this day and hour.

I looked into the Ark of Covenant to see what the Lord wanted to give me. Inside was the golden jar of manna. This represented provision to walk in the principles and kingdom of the Lord. To this point, the Lord had shown me tremendous financial increase in my life. It was not for me, but for His kingdom. I am committed to utilizing the majority of my resources for His kingdom here on earth and I set for myself increasing targets every year. This always reinforces the reality of who is in control of my life. There is nothing like being dependant on Him. My savings account on earth does not matter to me. My account in heaven is the one that matters.

The next thing inside the Covenant was Aaron's rod. It was budding. This means it was still maturing. This represented authority. I did not take that lightly. The Lord had given me mantels of authority to walk in. I cannot walk in these realms of authority in my own ability, but rather in the power and ability of the Holy Spirit in my life. I also believe that He is releasing to the complete church the things He released to me. I believe we can declare a thing and that it shall be established when it is aligned with His heavenly kingdom.

The third thing in the Ark of the Covenant was the tablets of the Ten Commandments, the ones Moses inscribed upon and gave to Israel. I felt the Lord was showing me that the church body had been trying to walk out these commandments in their own strength and that this was changing by the Spirit. I felt the Lord saying that many are trying to walk out the commandments under the letter of the Law rather than by the Spirit of the Lord, and that that day is quickly coming to an end. He desires to help us through His grace. The Bible says, *"If you love Me, keep My commandments"* (John 14:15, NKJV).

The issue is not about keeping the Law. It is about love. Pure and simple love is the key. In your strength, you can't obey the commandments. You can totally and completely obey Him under the love of God and the love of the Lord Jesus in your life. The vision completely overwhelmed me. God is so good, and I believe that under a manifested heaven these three aspects of the kingdom are being released for you and me. He simply says to expect it by faith. This will radically revolutionize and transform your life if you receive it into your heart and walk in it. It has already been released for you, and I am excited about your future.

A Nation's Call

The Lord gave me a dream on December 23, 2009. Cathryn and I were in the dream. We were in an old house on the prairies of Canada, a house very draughty with one-pane glass windows. Because of the old structure of the building, the heat went through the ceiling. Cathryn was cooking in the kitchen, which also contained old fixtures. Everything looked incredibly old. I was talking to her in the kitchen when all of a sudden the kitchen went from old to new instantaneously. The new kitchen represents a new wineskin being released. Our house guest in the vision was a well-known prophet who has been with us a number of times. This prophet was in the family room right beside the kitchen. I said to him, "What in the world is going on?" The prophet confidently said, "Come with me and I will show you what is going on."

We walked outside. We were on a street in Australia. I was now looking down and I could see the two of us walking. I couldn't hear what we were saying, but we were conversing very intently, as if I was receiving critical instructions. Suddenly, we ran straight into a gentleman who had been in the RCMP with me about fifteen years ago. His name was Inspector Strongman. His wife was with him. The Lord showed me that seeing him was a good thing. We all shook each other's hands, but didn't share a word. Eighty percent of communication is body language. By shaking his hand, I knew that a confidence and authority was being released. I knew the Lord was ordaining and orchestrating a call to all the nations in that very instant of time and that strength and authority was being dispensed for prophetic ministry.

All of the dreams and visions the Lord has given me over this specific time period have been linked to an area concerning the advancement of the kingdom of heaven in one form or another on this earth. I believe that this release is upon us. They all came together in a one-month period. It was a mandate of heaven. It is not about you or me. It is about the kingdom of God advancing through your life. That is the message of the Gospel. It is not about getting you perfect; there is only one who is perfect—the Lord Jesus Christ. You can't change yourself, but He can. Your mandate is to love everyone. Jesus said on the cross, *"Father, forgive them, for they do not know what they do"* (Luke 23:34, NKJV).

CHAPTER NINE

Promises of God

Lose Your Mind

And Jesus having returned to Capernaum, after some days it was rumored about that He was in the house [probably Peter's]. And so many people gathered together there that there was no longer room [for them], not even around the door; and He was discussing the Word.

Then they came, bringing a paralytic to Him, who had been picked up and was being carried by four men. And when they could not get him to a place in front of Jesus because of the throng, they dug through the roof above Him; and when they had scooped out an opening, they let down the [thickly padded] quilt or mat upon which the paralyzed man lay. And when Jesus saw their faith [their confidence in God through Him], He said to the paralyzed man, Son, your sins are forgiven [you] and put away [that is, the penalty is remitted, the sense of guilt removed, and you are made upright and in right standing with God].

Now some of the scribes were sitting there, holding a dialogue with themselves as they questioned in their hearts, Why does this Man talk like this? He is blaspheming! Who can forgive sins [remove guilt, remit the penalty, and bestow righteousness instead] except God alone? And at once Jesus, becoming fully aware in His spirit that they thus debated within themselves, said to them, Why do you argue (debate, reason) about all this in your hearts? Which is easier: to say to the paralyzed man, Your sins are forgiven and put away, or to say, Rise, take up your sleeping pad or mat, and start walking about [and keep on walking]? But that you may know positively and beyond a doubt that the Son of Man has right and authority and power on earth to forgive sins— He said to the paralyzed man, I say to you, arise, pick up and carry your sleeping pad or mat, and be going on home.

And he arose at once and picked up the sleeping pad or mat and went out before them all, so that they were all amazed and recognized and praised and thanked God, saying, We have never seen anything like this before! (Mark 2:1–12)

Every miracle that Jesus did in the scripture He is still doing today. This is the story of Jesus healing a paralyzed man. The miracle was performed in Capernaum. After Jesus had been "punted" from Nazareth, he set up headquarters in Capernaum on the Sea of Galilee. Jesus would leave Capernaum and come back at different times. People were constantly keeping their eyes on Him. They understood His ministry, but did not embrace it.

The scripture says, *"And when they could not get Him to a place in front of Jesus because of the throng, they dug through the roof above Him; and when they had scooped out an opening, they let down the [thickly padded] quilt or mat upon which the paralyzed man lay."* To get things from God, you have to be determined. In the scripture they anticipated the supernatural. Matthew, Mark, and Luke all recorded this miracle. It is not a fairy tale. It actually happened. Jesus is the same yesterday, today, and forever. I know, it is hard to wrap your mind around this. When I see a good friend who is in the medical profession, I say, "I am trying to lose my mind." The reason I am trying to lose my mind is to gain the mind of Christ. The only one with a normal mind is Jesus. He had a mind able to hear the voice of the Father one hundred percent of the time. That is why the mind of Christ is so incredibly important to walking in a heavenly realm. I believe the mind of Christ is available for everyone who is a professing believer in the Lord. He had perfect communion with the Father.

"And when Jesus saw their faith [their confidence in God through Him], He said to the paralyzed man, Son, your sins are forgiven [you] and put away [that is, the penalty is remitted, the sense of guilt removed, and you are made upright and in right standing with God]." There was a real desperation to receive from the Lord. He saw their faith and

performed the miracle that was needed. He didn't see the chopping of the roof. To Jesus, this was faith. He said, "Your sins are forgiven." He didn't say, "You are healed." Have you thought about that? A sense of guilt was removed. Do you think that guilt and shame put people in sickness? There are theories that say arthritis is linked to bitterness. Can you imagine what anxiety, stress, and rage can do to you and your physical body?

North America is so different from the other parts of the world I have travelled to. In many places, you can't even see a doctor or receive any form of medical treatment. There is something about desperation that activates the power of God. Many people accept sickness because they are not desperate enough to receive their healing. I am not saying this is the case in every situation, but it is easier in many cases to accept pain medication when you are struggling with a headache. On the other hand, I know doctors are used of the Lord to allow us to walk in health, and that is a fact; my life has been saved because of divine healing flowing in and through the medical profession.

We understand such a very small percentage of how the spirit, soul, and body function corporately together. The Bible it sickness as being related to sin: *"Afterward, when Jesus found him in the temple, He said to him, See, you are well! Stop sinning or something worse may happen to you"* (John 5:14). We need to get out of the mindset that everything is predetermined. There are many things in our bodies that we accept but shouldn't. Sickness is related to sin and our attitudes towards sin. *"For all have sinned and fall short of the glory of God"* (Romans 3:23, NKJV). If you think you are exempt from this, you are wrong. There is no condemnation in the Lord, but we need to be aware that our bodies are the temple of the Holy Spirit and treat ourselves accordingly. Do not be afraid to examine your heart in these matters and accept the Lord's direction.

Returning to Mark 2, the scribes said, *"Why does this Man talk like this? He is blaspheming! Who can forgive sins [remove guilt, remit the penalty, and bestow righteousness instead] except God alone?"* Every place Jesus went, people tried to get him off-track and focused on some lesser issue outside the will of the Father. This very thing will continue to happen in each and every believer's life. As much as we love people and do not wish to see anyone go through anything negative in their lives, in order to see heaven manifest in your life your focus must continually be on the Lord. I believe I am a carrier of this revelation and that the Lord has given me an ability to effectively communicate this reality to others. Not losing your focus is one of the most foundational keys to heaven being in your life. The focus must always be the Lord.

Matthew 6:33 says, *"But seek ye first the kingdom of God…"* (KJV). This is not just a nice biblical statement that we can choose to ignore. It is a fact. Circumstances and situations constantly try to get us off-track. We can manifest God, but we can also manifest the enemy.

Jesus turned to the scribes, sensing their thoughts: *"And at once Jesus, becoming fully aware in His spirit that they thus debated within themselves, said to them, Why do you argue (debate, reason) about all this in your hearts?"* He was fully aware. He knew exactly what was going on every place He went. There will always be naysayers trying to rob you and get you off-track. The reality is that you need to be focused on the Lord and His kingdom constantly. Jesus perceived it by the Spirit. Each and every person has the choice to believe or not believe in God. We need to continually press forward for more of Jesus in our lives. We need to perceive by the Spirit.

Jesus said to the paralyzed man, *"The Son of Man has right and authority and power on earth to forgive sins."* I find it very interesting how it says "Son of Man," and not "Son of God." He says this because He was God and purposefully came in the form of a man. Jesus was the first God in the flesh. He did and said what His Father told Him to, and therefore His complete being was in alignment with heaven on earth.

At one time, I was vacationing along the Sea of Cortez in Mexico. You couldn't swim in the sea because the waves were too intense. Our hotel was on the beach. When I was in my room, the patio door would vibrate from the force of the waves. The sound didn't affect my ability to stand, but it did affect the patio door. For me, this became a perfect illustration that heaven works differently than we do on earth.

Never underestimate what the Lord can do in any circumstance. I have found in my own life that the Lord desires for me only to release words that line up with heaven, and therefore I am very guarded for the most part in what I say on an ongoing basis. We have a little box called the mind. The Lord was giving me a demonstration with the patio door. I didn't feel the waves hitting the beach, but the door did. The Lord showed me that heaven is different from earth.

Jesus prays, *"Thy kingdom come. Thy will be done in earth, as it is in heaven"* (Matthew 6:10, KJV). The way we do things is the result of training we receive to walk in an earthly realm. In some cases, we must unlearn the natural to have the supernatural. Sound and light cause things to happen spiritually. I believe that many people are plagued by their past, and this shapes the way they see the Lord and His plans and purposes for their lives. This causes them to stumble in many ways. The Bible says, *"But he was wounded for our transgressions, he was bruised for our iniquities: the chastisement of our peace was upon him; and with his stripes we are healed"* (Isaiah 53:5, KJV). When the Bible says you are forgiven, you are forgiven!

> And you, Capernaum, are you to be lifted up to heaven? You shall be brought down to Hades [the region of the dead]! For if the mighty works done in you had been done in Sodom, it would have continued until today. But I tell you, it shall be more endurable for the land of Sodom on the day of judgment than for you. (Matthew 11:23–24)

In this scripture, Jesus speaks about Capernaum as a place where He was not received. This was the place where He performed the majority of His miracles. I find this very interesting. People are constantly looking for a sign, even though the Lord has performed miracles for generations. Miracles do not change hearts. They get attention, but it is up to the Lord to come change the heart. I see miracles every single day. I am one of them. I am a walking, talking, breathing miracle—and so are you. We are breathing and living. You can't tell me that isn't a miracle. The only time you think about breathing is when you are losing your breath, but each and every breath is a miracle. The scripture says that through Christ Jesus there are literally billions of miracles happening every second. How exciting is that revelation? There is so much in life that we take for granted. In reality. Christ is at work surrounding us with heaven.

Divine Inspiration from God

I believe in divine inspiration. No one is perfect. The Lord showed me that I can be divinely inspired. When light hits darkness, something changes. When the supernatural touches the natural, a change takes place. There is a constant back and forth movement from the natural to supernatural. As I have said before, "I do not believe in accidents; I believe in divine appointments."

There is a collision between the natural and supernatural taking place in the universal church. It occurs in our hearts and minds. Let's look at Cain and Abel, for example. One was led by supernatural revelation, and the other did what he thought was good to his own mind. In a manner of speaking, Cain had walked away from what he knew to be truth. You will always run into something when you walk away from truth in your life. The scriptures declare, *"And you shall know the truth, and truth shall set make free"* (John 8:32, NKJV). It is not about what you know; it is about the truth you know that sets men free. Revelation of truth is important to walking under a manifested heaven for your life. Things might look good, but is God in it? The natural and supernatural are different. One is infused by the Spirit and the other is not.

The battle between the natural and supernatural goes on in everyone's life. Often we will be opposed when we are on a supernatural journey. The Bible says, *"The kingdom of heaven suffereth violence, and the violent take it by force"* (Matthew 11:12, KJV). This scripture is there for a reason.

> And the Lord opened the mouth of the donkey, and she said to Balaam, What have I done to you that you should strike me these three times? And Balaam said to

the donkey, Because you have ridiculed and provoked me! I wish there were a sword in my hand, for now I would kill you! And the donkey said to Balaam, Am not I your donkey, upon which you have ridden all your life long until this day? Was I ever accustomed to do so to you? And he said, No.

Then the Lord opened Balaam's eyes, and he saw the Angel of the Lord standing in the way with His sword drawn in His hand; and he bowed his head and fell on his face.

And the Angel of the Lord said to him, Why have you struck your donkey these three times? See, I came out to stand against and resist you, for your behavior is willfully obstinate and contrary before Me. And the ass saw Me and turned from Me these three times. If she had not turned from Me, surely I would have slain you and saved her alive. Balaam said to the Angel of the Lord, I have sinned, for I did not know You stood in the way against me. But now, if my going displeases You, I will return. The Angel of the Lord said to Balaam, Go with the men, but you shall speak only what I tell you. So Balaam went with the princes of Balak.

When Balak heard that Balaam had come, he went out to meet him at the city of Moab on the border formed by the Arnon [River], at the farthest end of the boundary. Balak said to Balaam, Did I not [earnestly] send to you to ask you [to come] to me? Why did you not come? Am not I able to promote you to honor? And

Balaam said to Balak, Indeed I have come to you, but do I now have any power at all to say anything? The word that God puts in my mouth, that shall I speak. (Numbers 22:28–38)

"And the Lord opened the mouth of the donkey." The Lord uses everything. This scripture is talking about the prophet Balaam, who was a prophet from Moab, a non-Israelite nation. The Moabites had a king named Balak who feared the Israelites, who were on their way to invade Moab. Balak therefore asked Balaam for help. The interaction here between the Moabites and the Israelites is interesting. Like Israel, the church is called to be an offensive invasion force for His kingdom. Quite literally, we are a force for Him. The Lord completely sanctions His church as a spiritual force bringing transformation and change to the natural realm. There is coming a day when the church and the Holy Spirit will be removed from this natural realm. When this removal occurs, the true ungodly nature of lawlessness will be demonstrated on the earth.

We have a spiritual inheritance and possessions in the unseen realm. The Lord desires us to take the spiritual realm. We are invaders who need to go in and occupy by the Spirit. Do you know what church means? It means "the taken out ones." You are no longer in the world, but you are a part of the world. This may appear to be a contradiction, but the Lord always moves in opposition to the natural realm.

All of heaven moves differently than the natural realm does. One clear example of this is in Proverbs 11:24–25, which says, *"There is one who scatters, yet increases more; and there is one who withholds more than is right, but it leads to poverty"* (NKJV). This scripture refers to anything we sow. If we sow finances, our finances will increase. If we sow love, love will increase. If we sow mercy, mercy will increase in our lives. I pray that you catch this reality by the Spirit of the Lord to see heaven advance in your life.

There is a realm called "the bride." The bride comes out of the church. Not everyone in the church is going to be in the bride. Those walking in their spiritual inheritance will be in the bride.

The kingdom of God needs to be in the church. The church is called to be spiritual. The reality is that there is a natural component occupying some ground. I am not talking about flesh and blood; I am talking about principalities, powers, and rulers of darkness. There is a battle to be spiritual, as opposed to natural. It may seem easier to be natural than supernatural. The Israelites were invading the Moabites. In other words, the supernatural was invading the natural. This made Balak nervous, so he called upon Balaam to prophesy and curse Israel. Balaam accurately prophesied the coming of the Lord Jesus Christ, and was unable to curse Israel. Balaam was a prophet of God who was being influenced by the natural. Three times, he could not curse Israel. There is a steady battle between the natural and the supernatural.

God Doesn't Change His Mind

The Lord is always the winner in a battle. The spiritual will invade the natural. It won't happen when you necessarily think it will. When the Lord does something, my advice is: "Get in, get out, or get run over." As part of the church body, we are called to invade the natural. Don't be nervous. Heaven's army is behind you. The devil wants to intimidate you right out of the Promised Land. We need to declare that we will not drop the ball. In the scripture, Balaam, who was supposed to hear from

God, heard first from the donkey. The donkey saw and heard before the prophet.

God let Balaam do things He knew were detrimental. God gave him instruction, but he took a different course. He hoped God would change His mind, but God cannot change His mind. We can't put God in a little box. His ways are not our ways. *"Jesus Christ (the Messiah) is [always] the same, yesterday, today, [yes] and forever (to the ages)"* (Hebrews 13:8). He does not change His mind. It also says in the Bible, *"But He was wounded for our transgressions, He was bruised for our iniquities; the chastisement for our peace was upon Him, and by His stripes we are healed"* (Isaiah 53:5, NKJV). He won't change His mind about your healing. It says, *"By his stripes you are healed"*—and you are healed. It's just a matter of time.

When we are in battle, we need to stand in the promises of God. When He says it, I believe it. There is a natural realm that doesn't believe in healing. The Lord is the one who brings it all together. We cannot back down because things look bad. God will fulfill his promises.

CHAPTER TEN

River of Gold

One day recently, while communing with the Lord, His Spirit brought me in a vision to a massive river. It was not a river of water; it was a river of gold flowing from the throne room of heaven. This gold was not about finances, although I recognize that gold clearly represents wealth. This was a different wealth. There was gold for every believer. The gold represented love, and He was about to release a massive river of it for believers to make it possible for us to truly love as He loves. Truly loving our enemies is one major aspect that Christians truly struggle with. Get ready, because under a manifested heaven this will all come to an end. Loving our enemies will become easy by the Spirit.

The Lord showed me three distinct attributes of the river that applies to every believer:

1. Humility

2. Compassion

3. Gratitude

Whoever will humble himself therefore and become like this little child [trusting, lowly, loving, forgiving] is greatest in the kingdom of heaven. (Matthew 18:4)

Humility

Humility is a part of the kingdom of God. When you start to think you are really good at something, you are in trouble. When you are doing things in your own strength, you are moving away from humility. The Lord is the one doing everything right in your life. Success may be an attribute you would like to have. If you have the Lord Jesus Christ in your heart and in your life, you are successful. Your success should not be measured by worldly standards; it should be measured in Godly standards.

There is no such thing as a self-made man. That would be a reality outside of God. *"Whoever will humble himself therefore and become like this little child [trusting, lowly, loving, forgiving] is greatest in the kingdom of heaven."* This means we have to humble ourselves. We are now in the end times, and we need to get lower every day. In order to do this, we need to press in. Humility is an attribute of love.

For example, quite a few years ago the pastor of a ministry was asked to sign documents over to a specific person. The pastor did this. He knew what was going on. He knew that he had rights, but he didn't defend them. He signed the ministry he had raised up over to someone else. He did this out of a heart of humility and it brought transformation and change. At time, we have all felt that our rights have been trampled on. Have you ever been on the highway and someone flies by you at 130 km/h when you are going 122km/h? You think to yourself, *Someone needs to get them.* We often believe our rights are being abused and try putting ourselves forward. Jesus died once to His own will. He died a second time physically on the cross, but He died to His own will when He was in the Garden.

When I was directed into ministry over twenty years ago, I was propelled into it; it wasn't by my choosing to do it. I felt much like Moses when he was chosen to be the deliverer of Israel, totally incapable in myself. At that time, I was falsely attacked. I chose to shut up and not say anything. People would come to me and ask why I wasn't defending myself. I knew I didn't have to defend myself. I knew the Lord had put me in ministry. Once I took the stand that I would shut up and not defend myself, miracles started happening. The key was humility. Sometimes it is more important to keep your mouth shut than to say something. You may think you have all the facts about a situation, but then you make judgments based on your assumptions. The reality is that you never have all of the facts before you. The key sometimes is to just to shut up!

> Whoever exalts himself [with haughtiness and empty pride] shall be humbled (brought low), and whoever humbles himself [whoever has a modest opinion of himself and behaves accordingly] shall be raised to honor. (Matthew 23:12)

It is so important to give up your agenda and realize that you are an instrument of the Lord Jesus Christ. Many ministries have stumbled and fallen. I grieve over them. They think they have something to offer outside of the Lord Jesus. I am not trying to act dignified, but in the church I pastor all I want is the Lord Jesus. However He comes, I embrace it.

> But He gives us more and more grace (power of the Holy Spirit, to meet this evil tendency and all others fully). That is why He says, God sets Himself against the proud and haughty, but gives grace [continually] to the lowly (those who are humble enough to receive it). (James 4:6)

There is an evil tendency in humanity and we are not exempt from this. We can become haughty, prideful, and somehow think that we have done something. This tendency is in all of us. The only way to fight it is through the Spirit of the Lord. God will set himself against you if you carry pride. In the end times humility is an attribute for the kingdom of God and his love. "For God so loved the world that He gave His only begotten Son, that whoever believes in Him should not perish but have everlasting life," (John 3:16 NKJV) How did Abraham stand over his first born son with a knife? He could only do this through God.

> Therefore humble yourselves [demote, lower yourselves in your own estimation] under the mighty hand of God, that in due time He may exalt you. (1 Peter 5:6)

Don't look for a promotion. Promotions come from the Lord. This scripture uses the word "demote." Demotion also may come from the

Lord. Our own estimation can never be too low. The Lord is the one that exalts. There are many successful people in the church as a body. They don't need to go around and flaunt it. They just do what they do every single day. Humility is the key.

Compassion

Have you ever heard of Rolland and Heidi Baker? Both Rolland and Heidi run Iris Ministries. with their headquarters in Mozambique, Africa. Heidi tells a story about a guy who was an alcoholic and did not bathe. She loved this guy day in and day out. One day, he smashed a bottle and put it to her neck. She just kept saying to him, "I love you." He fought against this love. Eventually, he got saved. Both Rolland and Heidi have story after story about the love of the Lord being supernaturally released through their ministry. I've had many people pull knives and guns on me. I have always been ready to take them out. Of course, this was before I was a pastor.

The compassion of God is so good. Jesus saw something in you and me. It was so compelling that He went to the cross on our behalf. You may be thinking that in some way humanity, or even you, is not worth of such a sacrifice. We need to understand that the Lord's heart is for each and every one of us. He desires to empower and equip us for His kingdom purposes. We need spiritual eyes to see what the Lord is doing.

> When He saw the throngs, He was moved with pity and sympathy for them, because they were bewildered (harassed and distressed and dejected and helpless), like sheep without a shepherd. (Matthew 9:36, AMP)

This scripture propelled me to pastor at the church I am at today. It caused me to say yes to the offer. It wasn't for the money. People said I was nuts to do it. I said to the Lord, "If you can do it, I can do it." Having compassion for people is an attribute that comes from the throne room of God. I am still processing it and possessed by the Lord in achieving this realm. Everyone has a need. The body of Christ can fulfill that need. Move in faith despite the need. The Lord will bring his compassion.

> Because when they knew and recognized Him as God, they did not honour and glorify Him as God or give Him thanks. But instead they became futile and godless in their thinking [with vain imaginings, foolish reasoning, and stupid speculations] and their senseless minds were darkened. (Romans 1:21)

It is so important to have a grateful heart. North American Christians are blessed in many ways. You may be going through a struggle right now, but if we were to compare ourselves to the rest of the world, we would see the blessing of the Lord upon us. I have personally seen many other societies and cultures. I think sometimes we need to go out more to see how blessed we are and how much we have. We need to be grateful. When you give up your thankfulness, you become futile and faithless. Our era seems to have a woe-is-me mentality. *"If anyone desires to come after Me, let him deny himself, and take up his cross daily, and follow Me"* (Luke 9:23, NKJV)

There is a battle happening inside of you. Your heart needs an emperor. Have you ever been in battle with your heart? There is a real battle happening inside of you. The Bible says, *"For let not that man suppose that he will receive anything from the Lord; he is a double-minded man, unstable in all his ways"* (James 1:7–8, NKJV). The double-minded man gets nothing. We need double-mindedness far from our lives. The definition of insanity is doing the same thing over and over expecting different results. This is also double-mindedness. You need to be fixed and focused on the Lord.

Gratitude

The third and final aspect of this chapter is having a grateful heart, a heart full of thanksgiving in whatever circumstance of life we find ourselves in.

Onwards from Deuteronomy 28:47, the Lord actually rebukes Israel for walking ungratefully towards Him. This aspect of ungratefulness was so prevailing that the Lord chose to punish Israel by subjecting them to serve the other nations of the world of their day. Could a grateful heart be the key for each and every one of us? The answer is an obvious yes if we want to have a manifested heaven in our lives.

In Philippians 4, Paul outlines his heart of gratefulness when he speaks of being content in every realm of life—both in the times when he had and when he did not have. The attribute of gratitude flows from the heavenly realm and is to be a key component of our lives.

The three attributes of the golden river in my vision were humility, compassion, and gratitude. Walking in these ways will bring real change in your life. You may feel that you have a lack in these areas. It is the Lord's grace that gives them to us. When I saw the river, it was increasing and it was available for all. The Lord says, "Just jump in and see what My Spirit can do for each of you." The decision has to come from our hearts. Then the Holy Spirit can work in these ways.

CHAPTER ELEVEN

Seeds of Discrepancy

I was once working out at a gym in Jerusalem. I was on the elliptical trainer, which works muscles in your arms and legs simultaneously. Usually I do a 30–35 minute workout on this particular machine before moving onto other aspects in my workout.

I was at the twenty-minute mark on this machine when a young lady got on the elliptical machine beside me. She was observing my efforts. She looked over at me and said something in Hebrew. After two attempts at starting a conversation, she realized that I was not paying attention to her. She began to speak louder.

Something suddenly went off inside my head and I realized she was talking to me. I looked at her and said, "Excuse me, I don't speak Hebrew. I only speak English." Then, in English, she said, "You may want to increase your stride."

I guess I wasn't going fast enough. I was soaking wet and could hardly speak without taking a deep breath. Yet this lady thought I needed to increase my stride. I thought to myself, *Oh my, I don't think I can.* I processed this for about a minute. I was hoping that I had made it to the end of my workout. I hadn't! I decided that I would try and do what this lady had suggested. I started to increase my stride. I was at 530 strides a minute and increased it to the maximum 650. I couldn't stride any faster; it was now at the maximum. Suddenly, much to my surprise, rather than the workout getting harder it started to feel easier. It was hard at the lower level and became easier at the higher level. I felt like I wasn't putting much effort into it, but I was getting better results.

I believe this experience brought a message for the church body. We have been labouring and sweating at a low intensity thinking we cannot go any higher or faster with the Lord. We don't think we can experience Him in a greater way. If we increase our intensity, things will get a lot easier—not harder, as we would expect. I believe that there are realms of glory we have yet to see that will rapidly come into view as we increase our stride.

New Fruit from Heaven

But God—so rich is He in His mercy! Because of and in order to satisfy the great and wonderful and intense love with which He loved us, [5]Even when we were dead (slain) by [our own] shortcomings and trespasses, He made us alive together in fellowship and in union with Christ; [He gave us the very life of Christ Himself, the same new life with which He quickened Him, for] it is by

grace (His favor and mercy which you did not deserve)
that you are saved (delivered from judgment and made
partakers of Christ's salvation). ⁶And He raised us up
together with Him and made us sit down together [giv-
ing us joint seating with Him] in the heavenly sphere
[by virtue of our being] in Christ Jesus (the Messiah, the
Anointed One). (Ephesians 2:4–6)

Not all dreams and visions are from the Lord. Without a doubt,
some are; one-third of the Bible is comprised of dreams and visions.
At the church I pastor, we have morning prayer. It is easy during these
times to have visitations from the Lord. We often see tremendous things
and have lots of fun with the Lord as a result of being in His presence.

I had a vision one morning that related to what had happened in
Jerusalem. I was at a banqueting table with the Lord. We were carrying
on a conversation while eating finger foods. We were laughing and having a great time. All of a sudden, the Lord Jesus took a piece of fruit and
handed it to me. He said, "Take a bite."

I looked at it and did not recognize what it was. I am the type of
person who likes to eat what I like, and I must absolutely recognize it
before eating anything. If it is unfamiliar I will not eat it.

I started to give my objections. Jesus looked at me, smiled, and said,
"Take the fruit."

I took it and ate it. It was the very best thing I had ever eaten. The
message was that the Lord is presenting us with new fruit, fruit that has
never been experienced or eaten before.

He who overcomes (is victorious), I will grant him
to sit beside Me on My throne, as I Myself overcame

(was victorious) and sat down beside My Father on His throne. ²²He who is able to hear, let him listen to and heed what the [Holy] Spirit says to the assemblies (churches). (Revelation 3:21–22)

The human lives within the confines of time, which was essentially created for us by the Lord. He is in no way restricted by time, and everything He does transcends time, although His actions affect each of us in a realm of time. You can live up to a hundred twenty years, but people often live for less. God is not confined by time. Time is for us. God knows the beginning to the end. It is all the same to Him. To God, a day is like a thousand years and a thousand years is like a day. The Bible says, *"Before I formed you in the womb I knew you; before you were born I sanctified you; I ordained you a prophet to the nations"* (Jeremiah 1:5, NKJV). This means He already knows the outcome of your life. He knows the choices you will make before you make them. He knows where you are and where you are headed. This is not something our natural mind can figure out. God is omnipresent. I go to heaven every day. *"Thy kingdom come. Thy will be done in earth, as it is in heaven"* (Matthew 6:10, KJV). Heaven can invade earth. It is a spiritual law. As believers, we know very little about what the Lord can do.

There is a new flow of the Holy Spirit we have never experienced before. It is available to you and me. The Lord is bringing us to new realms. I don't want the same old, same old. I don't want church; I want Him. The Lord is telling us that our strides need to be faster, in order for it to get easier. We are going to be experiencing things we have never experienced before. The Lord handed me that fruit. I had never seen it or tasted it before., but it was better than I could have ever imagined. This is what the Lord desires for us.

Two Seeds

There are two types of seeds—one is good, and the other is bad. The Word of God is a good seed. Humans are seeds—some are good and others are bad. Have you ever heard the reference to a bad apple? It is bad because of its seed. Jesus was a seed, and therefore we are seeds. The devil tries to take out good seed. That is why opposition and turmoil should not frighten you. The enemy wants you out of the race.

> And I will put enmity. Between you and the woman, And between your seed and her Seed; He shall bruise your head, and you shall bruise His heel. (Genesis 3:15, NKJV)

God is speaking in this scripture about what He is going to do. In the third line of the verse, the word "seed" is capitalized. God had a plan from the very beginning. It dealt with a seed. I find it interesting that men don't make seeds, women do. It is her seed infused with heaven.

I believe that Cain was not a good seed. The Bible says, *"If you do well, will you not be accepted? And if you do not do well, sin lies at the door. And its desire is for you, but you should rule over it"* (Genesis 4:7, NKJV). Cain completely left God's presence and went to live in Nod, which was east of Eden. I don't understand how he could have done that. I need the presence of God. He is the one that sustains me. With Cain and Abel, different seeds did different things. One wanted the presence of God, and the other went away from it. In fact, the bad seed tried to destroy the good one and to a certain extent succeeded, causing the Lord to introduce another good seed.

> And Adam's wife again became pregnant, and she bore a son and called his name Seth. For God, she said, has appointed for me another child instead of Abel, for Cain slew him. (Genesis 4:25)

God appointed another seed. His name Seth. If Cain was still around, why did He do this? I believe it was because the good seed was killed. There have to be two seeds—a good and a bad. In the world, there are always two seeds opposing each other.

> Another parable He set forth before them, saying, The kingdom of heaven is like a man who sowed good seed in his field. [25]But while he was sleeping, his enemy came and sowed also darnel (weeds resembling wheat) among the wheat, and went on his way. [26]So when the plants sprouted and formed grain, the darnel (weeds) appeared also. [27]And the servants of the owner came to him and said, Sir, did you not sow good seed in your field? Then how does it have darnel shoots in it? [28]He replied to them, An enemy has done this. The servants said to him, Then do you want us to go and weed them out? [29]But he said, No, lest in gathering the wild wheat (weeds resembling wheat), you root up the [true] wheat along with it. [30]Let them grow together until the harvest; and at harvest time I will say to the reapers, Gather the darnel first and bind it in bundles

to be burned, but gather the wheat into my granary.
(Matthew 13:24–30)

Jesus loved parables. He would tell them to His disciples while demonstrating the power of God in all that He did. This parable demonstrated His kingdom. Whatever you sow in the kingdom, you will reap in the kingdom. You are a good seed. It is important to remember that the enemy sows bad seeds, and in the Bible there are a lot of them. If we take out the bad weed, do some of the good weeds have to go to? This is the point I am trying to make. The Lord is bringing us into the harvest and there is new fruit.

> Then He left the throngs and went into the house. And His disciples came to Him saying, Explain to us the parable of the darnel in the field. [37]He answered, He Who sows the good seed is the Son of Man. [38]The field is the world, and the good seed means the children of the kingdom; the darnel is the children of the evil one, [39]And the enemy who sowed it is the devil. The harvest is the close and consummation of the age, and the reapers are angels. [40]Just as the darnel (weeds resembling wheat) is gathered and burned with fire, so it will be at the close of the age. (Matthew 13:36–40)

The disciples went to Jesus and said they didn't understand the parable of the wheat and darnel. Jesus explained it to them. You are a child of the Most High God. There is a distinction coming between one seed and the other. I believe we are so close to this taking place. Will you take the fruit the Lord has for you? He has ordained it.

It is as Isaiah predicted, If the Lord of hosts had not left us a seed [from which to propagate descendants], we [Israel] would have fared like Sodom and have been made like Gomorrah. (Romans 9:29)

If the Lord does not leave His seed within humanity, every form of corruption will come. The seed of God is here today. There is something holding back the power of the adversary right now. It is the Holy Spirit. There is a time coming when this adversary will be unleashed in this world. The only thing that will sustain the church body is the Lord Jesus Christ in His seed. We need Him in our hearts and our lives. He needs to be our priority.

CHAPTER TWELVE

Significance of the Heavenly Word

Don't Despise the Fire

When I was a young child, I had a traumatic experience with a barber. I had a wart on the back of my neck. I went into the barber, and when I left the wart was gone. I didn't know how it even happened. Now, once a month, like clockwork, I get my hair cut by my barber, Terry. When my hair gets long and touches my ear, I know it's time to go in. Terry talks with me about his potato mounds and it takes fifteen minutes to cut my hair. On one routine occasion, he got out his razor said two words to me—"Shave around."

I believe we are in a critical time and hour. The Lord is getting out his razor and shaving around us to a razor thin edge. This is happening in the body of Christ. What has been acceptable in the past is not acceptable anymore. A shaving is taking place, and the Lord is doing it. Many prophetic words state that the fire will come. Don't despise the fire; out of fire comes the purity of the Lord. The refiner's fire produces something if you allow the Holy Spirit to work.

I do not see myself as a pastor. It is the function I fulfill. The reality is that I am not a hireling. I am not hired to do a specific function. I don't work for anyone; I work for the Lord. I don't view ministry the way most do. I am only interested in the mandate of heaven and it is only out of this flow that I can function as a minister of the Gospel. Anyone used of the Lord has this mandate on their life. These people are kingdom-focused and do not focus on people issues. They purpose to achieve something for the kingdom of God. This mandate is on each and every believer. You are created for a purpose, for total communion with God to advance His kingdom here on earth.

Over fourteen years ago, the Lord gave my wife and me a charge to the ministry I pastor to this day. All authority comes from God. That ministry started with nineteen people. I got a call from a man named Randy Neilson, who asked if I would be interested in coming to Sylvan Lake for a few weeks to preach to these nineteen people. I agreed, and after the two weeks I got another call. I was asked to preach for two more weeks, and I accepted. A pastor had actually been hired on Sunday, and by the following Monday he had quit.

I was asking the Lord what He wanted me to do. He brought me to a scripture and I decided that the Lord's hand was upon me taking authority for this body of believers. It was only the result of a word the Lord had given me that propelled me into ministry. Over the years, this authority and the way I received it has become a strength in my life.

You need to know that you are divinely appointed for the mandate of heaven in your life.

The Mandate of Heaven Rests on Your Life

> And Jesus went about all the cities and villages, teaching in their synagogues and proclaiming the good news (the Gospel) of the kingdom and curing all kinds of disease and every weakness and infirmity. [36]When He saw the throngs, He was moved with pity and sympathy for them, because they were bewildered (harassed and distressed and dejected and helpless), like sheep without a shepherd. [37]Then He said to His disciples, The harvest is indeed plentiful, but the laborers are few. [38]So pray to the Lord of the harvest to force out and thrust laborers into His harvest. (Matthew 9: 35–38)

This was the scripture the Lord gave me that propelled my wife and me into ministry. Storms will always try to come against the mandate of heaven in your life. Initially, Cathryn wanted nothing to do with my decision to move to Sylvan Lake, but the Lord moves on hearts and it was to be shortly confirmed to her.

In this scripture, Jesus is speaking the Gospel of the kingdom. As believers, we are all called to be equipped in the ministry of the Lord Jesus Christ—in essence, we are to be mini Christs on this earth. The Lord saw *"sheep without a shepherd."* He was moved by compassion, and He moved on my heart. *"The harvest is indeed plentiful, but the laborers are few."* Whatever the mandate of heaven is in your life, it will come with opposition. Jesus was opposed. People don't oppose you; the enemy is the opposition. We do not wrestle against flesh and blood. It is important to always remember this fact.

Jesus prayed in the Garden and said, *"Father, if You are willing, remove this cup from Me; yet not My will, but [always] Yours be done"* (Luke 22:42). Jesus went to the cross because He wanted to advance the kingdom which was directly opposed to His natural will. In the Bible, Jesus said, *"If anyone desires to come after Me, let him deny himself, and take up his cross daily, and follow Me"* (Luke 9:23, NKJV). This means you should not feel sorry for yourself when trying circumstances come your way. You have a cross that you need to pick up daily for Him.

> Then Mary said, Behold, I am the handmaiden of the Lord; let it be done to me according to what you have said. And the angel left her. (Luke 1:38)

It is a critical time, and we are in a critical hour. All of us have been impregnated with the kingdom of God. I can't imagine the conversation between Mary and Joseph when she explained what had happened to her—"An angel came to me and now I am pregnant." Try putting yourself in that position. Joseph had a heart for Mary, but he also had to see through his spiritual eyes. How would you have reacted if you were Joseph?

We are in a critical time and hour. Many will fall if they do not see through their spiritual eyes. I am like Mary, pregnant. The mandate of heaven rests on my life and your life, and the Lord will use us I to advance His kingdom out of a heart of love. The mandate of heaven rests on your life. You just need eyes to see it.

False Accusations

> Until the time that his word came to pass, The word of
> the Lord tested him. (Psalms 105:19)

I had revelation on this scripture many years ago. It is one of my favourites. Joseph got a word from the Lord. As soon as he did, his world became a series of ups and downs. He was falsely accused. False accusations are a threat from the devil. False accusations happen to those who are advancing the kingdom of God, so expect them to come your way.

CHAPTER THIRTEEN

Snowy Days

The presence of God is totally and completely what I am after for myself and for you. Through the presence of the Holy Spirit lives are changed and transformed. Without God and His presence, nothing can be done in our lives. I am hungry to go deeper with Him.

I once had the opportunity to minister in Mozambique, Africa. Incredible things are happening there by the Spirit of the Lord. One thing I felt the Lord show me was that the missionaries and staff needed more of the presence of the Lord in their lives. We all do. I was not trying to judge; we truly all need greater levels of the Spirit of the Lord. At times, I feel very weak in my body. I have nothing to give naturally. Spiritually, I have a lot to give.

Be Led by the Spirit

> Benaiah son of Jehoiada, whose father was a valiant
> man of Kabzeel, had done mighty deeds. He slew the
> two sons of Ariel of Moab. Also he went down and slew
> a lion in a pit in time of snow. (1 Chronicles 11:22)

This scripture talks about Benaiah going in a pit on a snowy day to kill a lion. You may not know it, but you have slayed many in the Spirit if you are walking by the Spirit of the Lord. Even on a snowy day you can have a divine appointment.

One day, I was backing out of my garage. There was about five inches of snow on the ground. The first thought that came to me was, *I should have shovelled the snow today.* I felt led by the Spirit of the Lord to let it melt. You may be faced with a lion on a snowy day, but you need to be led by the Spirit of the Lord.

The kingdom of God is advancing. The mandate of heaven for us is to advance the kingdom of God. It is not something for you to do alone. It is up to you and me to carry this mandate to the nations of the world. We need to purpose in our hearts to go everywhere the Lord wants us to go. Who cares if our bodies are weak and we are tired? By His Spirit, we can draw the strength we need. When we are weak, He is strong (2 Corinthians 12:10). We need to be where God wants us to be in the power that He provided for us.

Too many people don't have insight and understanding of the presence of God. It is not about words. Paul said that the kingdom of God does not advance through eloquence of words, but by the demonstration of power by the Spirit of God (1 Corinthians 10:17). Demonstration are manifestations of the kingdom of God. The Greek definition of manifesting means "unfolding." We need an unfolding in our lives by the presence of God. It can't be done in our strength. *"My grace is sufficient for you, for My strength is made perfect in weakness"* (2 Corinthians 12:9, NKJV).

Obedience to the Lord can only be achieved through His power. The power comes through a demonstration in our lives. Those who love Him, obey Him. Jesus was obedient unto His death. You are also called to obedience unto death. *"If anyone desires to come after Me, let him deny himself, and take up his cross daily, and follow Me"* (Luke 9:23, NKJV).

Satan and Christ have one thing in common—they both want you dead for very different reasons. The devil wants you dead because you are a threat. Jesus wants you dead to yourself so that the kingdom of God can take effect and see heaven advance in your life. Without the presence of God, it is all over. Things will come forward, but we cannot put any restrictions on the presence of God advancing in this nation. We need to continue to push behind anything advancing the kingdom of God.

We Need Revelation to Change

> Who has believed (trusted in, relied upon, and clung to) our message [of that which was revealed to us]? And to whom has the arm of the Lord been disclosed? (Isaiah 53:1)

As believers, we need to believe every word in the Bible. We cannot pick and choose what we like and don't like. They are all applicable. We need to have a revelation of every word. You are not able to walk the walk with my revelation or the revelation of great preachers like Joel

Olsteen or Jerry Seville. If the revelation doesn't come from within you, it won't affect you.

A lot of people say to the preacher, "Wow, that was a great word." I believe that if it doesn't bring change, it wasn't a great word. We need to be seeking after life-changing words. What revelation is to me might not be what it is to you. That's where love needs to kick in. We need to have understanding and love for everyone, no matter where they are at. Your revelation or words will not bring forth change upon anyone, but love through your words will. Affirmation comes when people come into agreement with each other. It pushes us forward.

In church, something happens when we hold our hands up. Revelation comes. The first time I held my hands up in church, I got a migraine headache. In all honesty, I know it was because a demon was coming off me. When we have breakthroughs, something goes from our lives and we are totally transformed by the Holy Spirit. Now I can lift my hands and feet, too—but not at the same time!

Do you have a promise from the Lord? Are you clinging to it? You may have had a promise for great increase, but have forgotten it. You may have seen everything but increase in your life. The Lord will sometimes remind us of these promises. I have not seen the total results of some promises in my life, but I still cling to them. It is important to stand and cling to all promises from the Lord. If it came from the throne room of God, He will do it. In our own strength, we cannot make it happen. We are weak, but the Holy Spirit is strong.

The timing is not ours. We need to declare that we will not abort the destiny and promises over our lives. A key word in Isaiah 53:1 is "revealed." When the Lord reveals something to you, run with it. It is not about the strength we have within us, but His strength.

A Revelation Is Taking Place

> At that time Jesus began to say, I thank You, Father,
> Lord of heaven and earth [and I acknowledge openly
> and joyfully to Your honor], that You have hidden these
> things from the wise and clever and learned, and re-
> vealed them to babies [to the childish, untaught, and
> unskilled]. [26]Yes, Father, [I praise You that] such was
> Your gracious will and good pleasure. [27]All things have
> been entrusted and delivered to Me by My Father and
> no one fully knows and accurately understands the Son
> except the Father, and no one fully knows and accur-
> ately understands the Father except the Son and anyone
> to whom the Son deliberately wills to make Him known.
> (Matthew 11:25–27)

These are the words of the Lord Jesus. It is important that we understand them. The Lord Jesus revealed hidden things to babies and children who were untaught. I have a degree, but that means nothing to the Lord. In order to have success in life, we need to gain revelation from God. I would rather have wisdom and understanding than all the degrees in the world. Your mind works against revelation. Your mind is enmity to God. It works against Him. There is a war going on in your mind. Not everyone will understand the scriptures in the Bible. Only the Holy Spirit can reveal the truth so we can understand it for our lives. Have you ever cooked with an onion? There are many layers of an onion. As you peel through the many layers, it gets whiter and whiter. There is a process of revelation that takes place, and it can come layered as we seek the Lord.

It's Time for a Heavenly Invasion

In the Bible it says, *"All things have been delivered to Me by My Father, and no one knows the Son except the Father. Nor does anyone know the Father except the Son, and the one to whom the Son wills to reveal Him"* (Matthew 11:27, NKJV). God became your Lord and Saviour by the revelation of His Son Jesus Christ. Out of the heart, your mouth spoke life into you. This is why the presence of God is so important in our lives. We need to be walking with the Holy Spirit a hundred percent of the time. I am not at that point myself. I purpose to have the percentage increase in my life each day. There is only one person who flowed in the Spirit one hundred percent, and it was Jesus. I am going after that.

> I assure you, most solemnly I tell you, if anyone steadfastly believes in Me, he will himself be able to do the things that I do; and he will do even greater things than these, because I go to the Father. And I will do [I Myself will grant] whatever you ask in My Name [as presenting all that I AM], so that the Father may be glorified and extolled in (through) the Son. ¹⁴[Yes] I will grant [I Myself will do for you] whatever you shall ask in My Name [as presenting all that I AM]. ¹⁵If you [really] love Me, you will keep (obey) My commands. (John 14:12–15)

This is our calling. How amazing would it be to go up to someone and say, "You live at this house, and you have this problem, and the Lord Jesus is healing it right now"? There have been forerunners in this area. This actually happens by the Spirit of the Lord. We are called to be a greater-works generation. We need a heavenly invasion. In the scripture, it says, *"Thy kingdom come. Thy will be done in earth, as it is in heaven"* (Matthew 6:10, KJV). We need to claim heaven on Earth.

Speak Life Over People

> And He said to them, Is the lamp brought in to be put under a peck measure or under a bed, and not [to be put] on the lampstand? [22][Things are hidden temporarily only as a means to revelation.] For there is nothing hidden except to be revealed, nor is anything [temporarily] kept secret except in order that it may be made known. [23]If any man has ears to hear, let him be listening and let him perceive and comprehend. [24]And He said to them, Be careful what you are hearing. The measure [of thought and study] you give [to the truth you hear] will be the measure [of virtue and knowledge] that comes back to you—and more [besides] will be given to you who hear. [25]For to him who has will more be given; and from him who has nothing, even what he has will be taken away [by force]. (Mark 4:21–25)

The Spirit of the Lord is in you. It is not meant to be hidden. From the start of becoming a Christian to wherever you are now, things have been revealed. The closer you get to Him, the greater the revelation that comes. As we draw near to Him, He will draw near to us. The Lord desires to reveal every secret in the scriptures to you. The Lord desires to show you heaven on earth. There will be opposition that will come with this, but do not give up. Be careful of what you are hearing. When you talk to people, speak life. When I talk to people, I speak life over them. Understand that this can only happen by the presence of God in your life to advance His kingdom.

When I was in Mozambique, I was trying to describe heaven to the African pastors who were gathered for training. As I was attempting to explain the concept of heaven, it became obvious to me that I was using terminology readily understood in Western culture, but not easily understood by those who had never experienced a cold climate. I felt the Lord say, "Describe what a snowy day in Alberta is like." I started to talk about where I was from and the fact that for six months of the year there is three feet of frozen snow piled up. I could tell by the expression on their faces that the analogies I was using were totally not being understood. They had never seen snow. They came from a climate with a hundred percent humidity and high temperatures all year round. In southern Africa, the second you come out of the shower, you need another one due to the overwhelming humidity. If you walk in a room with a lot of people, the smell of humanly produced perfume can knock you over. If you have been there, you will understand.

The enemy wants to destroy you. He will try causing you to undershoot the calling on your life. No one can "overshoot" heaven, by the way, although many may think they can become too holy or fanatical for the Lord. You can never be too holy, you can never be too pure, and you can never be too fanatical for the Lord! The Lord will never say, "Oh my, you are too holy."

Years ago, there was a tightrope walker who crossed Niagara Falls. As Christians, sometimes we like to walk on a tightrope around this issue. The grace of God has been released to you. There is new mercy for you. If you gain revelation and hear by the Spirit, more will be given to you. What the Lord has for you cannot be taken away. The scriptures tell us to either be hot or cold, but not lukewarm. Who will you serve this day?

CHAPTER FOURTEEN

The Clash of Two Systems

It is important to realize that there is a clash going on between two systems operating in your life. One system is rooted in faith and the other system is rooted in fear.

Divine Appointments

One time, I was in the city of Calgary with my wife Cathryn. We had stayed the night. The next morning, we jumped into my brand new vehicle to head home. I hit the gas and the vehicle wouldn't move an inch. Sure enough, the transmission had blown. My son lives in Calgary, so I borrowed his Mazda to get us home. As Cathryn and I were driving down the highway, we heard a rumble. I turned to Cathryn and said, "How can they drive this vehicle?" Suddenly, the tire blew. I saw pieces blowing all over the road. All the cars behind me were slamming on their breaks. Inside, the vehicle we were calm. We veered over to the side of the road. I got out and headed to the trunk to get the spare tire. Have you ever changed a tire with rusted lug nuts? We ended up having to call a tow truck. It turned out that the driver who came was from Red Deer, Alberta—the same city we hold our Saturday night services in. It was a divine appointment.

I had a meeting with a financial advisor awhile back. He told me that the banks in the United States recently could have completely failed. The reason for this was that people became fearful and were going to the bank to withdrawal all their money. The banks increased their insurance from $100,000 to $250,000. By doing this, people calmed down. This goes to show that there is a lot of fear in people. Often this fear controls what we do. There are two systems that control what we do—faith and fear.

In 1996, I had the opportunity to go to Russia and travel to a remote location in Siberia with a gentleman from Sweden named David Nystrom, a man of God. In the former Soviet Union and European countries, people congregate in public squares, and they have done so for centuries. It was there that people would hear the messages of the day. To a major extent, the Gospel of the kingdom advanced because of the message being communicated in these squares. Dave and I went into this Siberian community and sat in the community square with the intent through our translator of proclaiming the Gospel. Then, because of my background, I noticed that we were under surveillance and decided to leave the area. Before we could go, the police came to apprehend us. The charges brought against us were associated with proclaiming the Gospel of the kingdom, even though we had not uttered a word. It was against the law to share the Lord Jesus Christ in that community. They thought, "Here is a way to make a quick $500 off these guys."

We appeared before a magistrate, and I wondered if I would be interrogated. This gave me the opportunity to operate out of fear or faith. When the case was over, we paid a fine of $10 and were released. Even though fear had attempted to enter into our lives, both David and I moved into a new realm of faith in our risen Saviour. Have you ever been hit by fear? It's time to choose faith in whatever you are going through right now.

In July 2007, I went to Vietnam. In the receiving customs and immigration lounge, I was challenged in my heart as to whether my background would be a prohibition to my entrance into the nation, and I felt the Lord clearly say, "No, I have called you to be here and I am releasing a new realm of rest for you, even in this nation." I stood in line for two hours in searing heat prior to being admitted into the country. The same thought hit me: *Will I be interrogated?* I had been in Vietnam with a religious visa, and at the time our ministry fully more than twenty pastors on a monthly basis in Vietnam. I realized that life had very little value in much of the world human, and Vietnam was no exception, although the people there were very warm, friendly, and compassionate.

When I got to the front of the line, I looked at the guy who was working the border security booth and he looked back at me. Without a doubt in his mind, he stamped my passport. I was in the country. When I left the country, I went through the same line. The same border guard was working at the booth, and again without hesitation he stamped my passport. I believe this was another divine appointment.

We wrestle between faith and fear in our lives. These two systems are clashing constantly. The Lord is asking us to walk in a higher realm, a realm of faith. If we believe in divine healing, finances, and bigger things for our lives and those around us, we have to start changing from fear to faith. I often say, "Devil, give me your best shot!" We are not rooted on shifting sand. We are planted on solid rock. Solid rock cannot be shaken. What you have relied on in the past cannot be relied on in the future. Those who endure to the end will bear tremendous fruit.

> Because of faith Enoch was caught up and transferred to heaven, so that he did not have a glimpse of death; and he was not found, because God had translated him. For even before he was taken to heaven, he received testimony [still on record] that he had pleased and been satisfactory to God. ⁶But without faith it is impossible to please and be satisfactory to Him. For whoever would come near to God must [necessarily] believe that God exists and that He is the rewarder of those who earnestly and diligently seek Him [out]. (Hebrews 11:5–6)

Spiritually-Revealed Truth

How great would it be to walk with God and Him say "Let's go!"? Enoch had been satisfactory to God because of his faith. I believe that faith is spiritually-revealed truth that comes from the Word of God. How did you get saved? You were saved by spiritually-revealed truth. There are different levels of spiritually-revealed truth. If you ask the Lord for truth, He will not give you a stone. It is important to receive truth, and to know that only He can reveal it to you.

Therefore let us go on and get past the elementary stage in the teachings and doctrine of Christ (the Messiah), advancing steadily toward the completeness and perfection that belong to spiritual maturity. Let us not again be laying the foundation of repentance and abandonment of dead works (dead formalism) and of the faith [by which you turned] to God. (Hebrews 6:1)

Belief develops out of revelation. Our foundation is in Jesus Christ. There may be things in your life that you haven't seen come to pass. You may have fear overwhelming your life right now, and that is okay. God understands. There is a war constantly going on in all of us between faith and fear. You may believe for relationships to be restored, finances brought to order, healing in your life, or what step to take next—the Lord wants to release all of this to you.

CHAPTER FIFTEEN

The Master Builder

It's Okay to Dream

For about two years, I believed for a project to come together. The project was a retreat centre that could be used as a place of refuge. When people are being attacked, they would go there to hear from the Lord. I want to have a 24/7 house of prayer. This was the dream I believed the Lord for. One random Monday morning, someone representing a foundation came into my office. They sowed $10,000 into the ministries that I belong to. Now all that is left is to get the permits in place and get started. It's okay to dream. Don't drop it and keep going. All dreams can happen, by the Spirit of the Lord.

On June 6, 2010 was the sixty-sixth anniversary of the invasion of Normandy on D-Day. I believe this date is very strategic in the

Spirit. After great preparation and sacrifice, the first steps in the defeat of a major adversary were achieved. I believe there is a spiritual significance to this. A lot of preparation and detail was put in place. It looked like the Allies were going to lose the war up until this point, and an invasion of Great Britain was also anticipated. In relation to the cross, everything pointed to Christ being defeated. The disciples thought they were defeated. That's when God's plans kicked into overdrive. He knows what He is doing, even when we don't have a clue. I believe the enemy is on the run. What looked like the greatest defeat to the natural eye turned into the greatest victory for the kingdom of heaven.

There are a lot of things in the world that are incomplete. They are all around us. Do you ever feel incomplete or inadequate? The reality is that each and every one of us is incomplete until we are infused by the Holy Spirit. It's okay to feel inadequate and that you don't know what you are doing. The Bible says, *"But God has chosen the foolish things of the world to put to shame the wise, and God has chosen the weak things of the world to put to shame the things which are mighty"* (1 Corinthians 1:27, NKJV). God uses the things that people don't like to see. I am not enamoured by gifts. I am more enamoured with being surrendered, going lower, having a Christ-like character, and being humble. I want to be close to people who go after these qualities. Gifts are simply that—gifts.

> The earth was without form, and void; and darkness was on the face of the deep. And the Spirit of God was hovering over the face of the waters. (Genesis 1:2, NKJV)

Sometimes we may feel empty going through life day in and day out. You may ask the Lord, "Why am I here? What is this all about?" This is what we are constantly asking, whether we are aware of it or not. We think things like, *Why do I react this way? Why is there so much turmoil or chaos in the world?* A simple answer to these questions is that we are in the world, but we are not of the world. The reality is that each and every one of us is different. We are called to be heavenly invaders, making a difference in this lost and dying world.

One time, I went to visit a gentleman in the Red Deer hospital. I was in the room for five seconds on my second visit, when I asked him, "Do you want to accept the Lord?" He said, "Yes." His family had been trying to lead him to the Lord for years. It may have been God's plan to have someone else lead him to the Lord. He was saved and died three months later. I ended up being the minister at his funeral in Saskatchewan. I was a half-hour late and said, "He would be looking down on us, saying, 'This pastor would be late even for his own funeral.'"

The Holy Spirit's Renewal

The world's system is all about making us feel comfortable and safe. Things such as photo radar, traffic lights, and air conditioning all help make us comfortable. This helps to avoid turmoil and chaos. This may throw you off, but I believe there is a better way.

I am a pretty routine person. I am up at 5:00 a.m. and I am in the office shortly after. One winter morning, I was in my office shaving. The power was out and I had no light. I was a little ticked, but I felt the Lord say, "There will be a day when all these convenient things may not be available to you." I just kept shaving. We are too dependent on the world's systems. They are a safety net that we all rely on. One day they will come to an end, and the Holy Spirit better be leading you and instrumental in your life. The Bible says, *"Behold, I send you out as sheep in the midst of wolves. Therefore be wise as serpents and harmless as doves"* (Matthew 10:16, NKJV). It starts with our thinking. We need to let the Holy Spirit renew us.

> The earth was without form and an empty waste, and darkness was upon the face of the very great deep. The Spirit of God was moving (hovering, brooding) over the face of the waters. (Genesis 1:2)

Light penetrates darkness. Have you ever heard of quantum physics? Light and sound is the same thing. I was in a service once and my Bible started to vibrate on my lap. Sound was vibrating the scripture. There are so many things in life that we do not understand. When words are spoken, something happens. I am opposed to negative words. One time someone said to me, "I don't know if you are telling me the truth, or if you are just saying positive words." I said to them, "My positive words are the truth." If you do not think our words have an effect, you are wrong. They have more significance than you know. I choose to keep my mouth shut a lot. There are many words that I don't want to release.

Incubation by the Spirit

As it says in Genesis 1, *"The Spirit of God was moving."* The Spirit of God is continually moving. You may feel inadequate, incapable, weak, and as though you can't carry out the basic things of life. By the Spirit of the Lord, these things are possible. The Spirit was hovering and brooding, like a chicken over its eggs. The Spirit is like an incubator; it incubates and hovers. This is how we reach higher realms in our walk with the Lord.

> See, I have this day appointed you to the oversight of the nations and of the kingdoms to root out and pull down, to destroy and to overthrow, to build and to plant. (Jeremiah 1:10)

The mandate of heaven is contained in this scripture. The Lord only tears down so He can build back up. The Lord is the master builder in all things. Think of the Flood. The Lord destroyed everything to rebuild it all.

> For I will set My eyes upon them for good, and I will bring them again to this land; and I will build them up and not pull them down, and I will plant them and not pluck them up. ⁷And I will give them a heart to know (recognize, understand, and be acquainted with) Me, that I am the Lord; and they will be My people, and I will be their God, for they will return to Me with their whole heart. (Jeremiah 24:6–7)

The Lord will set his eyes upon you forever. In Psalms, it says, *"The righteous shall flourish like a palm tree"* (Psalms 92:12, NKJV). Many people attend church, but they are not planted. The Lord is calling us to be planted and flourished. It doesn't matter what church you are planted in. The important thing is being planted in a believing church. Storms will come and you need to have a solid foundation with the

Lord. The Lord wants your whole heart. He doesn't want anything else occupying your heart.

Three Kinds of Suffering

> And I tell you, you are Peter [Greek, Petros—a large piece of rock], and on this rock [Greek, petra—a huge rock like Gibraltar] I will build My church, and the gates of Hades (the powers of the infernal region) shall not overpower it [or be strong to its detriment or hold out against it]. (Matthew 16:18)

When you have a dream, all hell comes against it. When you focus on advancing the kingdom of God, all hell comes against it. In my life, since I have been focused on advancing the kingdom of God, there has been steady opposition. If the kingdom of God is advancing, it has to be a good thing. In the Bible, there is a distinct difference between good things and God things.

When I decided to go to Bible school, well-intended people told me, "You have a great career and you are doing well where you are at." That was all true. Well-intended people can be used of the enemy. These people are not the devil. They are simply not being mindful, like Peter, of the kingdom of God. Nobody wanted to see Jesus go to the cross. I would have felt the same way under the same reality, but our ways are not the Lord's ways—and that is a good thing. If you're honest, you wouldn't have desired for Christ to go to the cross, either. Unless we have the mind of Christ, things will usually not go the way we think.

We have a tendency to think only good things should be happening to us, but in reality the Lord uses it all to mould us into His image.

Sometimes we need to suffer. There are three types of suffering in the scripture. The first is suffering because we are in the world. The second is suffering because we are Christians. The third is suffering because there is sin in our lives. We only have control over one-third of these sufferings, and that is sin in our lives.

When Paul tried to go to Rome, he got shipwrecked along the way (Acts 27). He had divine purpose and he understood the mandate of heaven. God does not want us to despise the fires that are going on in and around our lives. The Lord is the master builder and He is building you and me. This is one way the kingdom of heaven advances in our hearts and lives. No one is immune from this aspect of the Gospel, but many choose to ignore it.

At times, there seems to be a mentality that everything should go well in every aspect of our lives. This is not in any way correct in doctrine. If you have a dream, let the Lord build it. If you keep your eyes on the master builder, it will be built. He knows exactly what to do. Each and every one of us carries a mandate. There will always be opposition. Remember that you are not an accident. You are here on divine assignment. Ridicule and mockery will try and get you off-track, but we need to see things the way the Lord sees them.

> And he said before his brethren and the army of Samaria, What are these feeble Jews doing? Will they restore things [at will and by themselves]? Will they [try to bribe their God] with sacrifices? Will they finish up in a day? Will they revive the stones out of the heaps of rubbish, seeing they are burned? (Nehemiah 4:2)

Nehemiah, one of the Old Testament prophets, had a mandate from heaven. He was asked to rebuild the temple and rebuild what had been torn down by the enemy in Jerusalem with the taking of the Jewish people into captivity in Babylon. The King of Persia asked Sanballat and Tobiah, authorities of the Persian Empire in Jerusalem, to help Nehemiah, and they were totally opposed to this rebuilding. Your adversary will not assist you in building, and in some cases your adversary may plant those around you who are in direct opposition to the plans and purposes of God, simply because they are not mindful of the kingdom of God for your life. The name Sanballat means "god of sin being glorified." The territory had belonged to the Israelites. The Israelites were coming back and the people who were there were opposed.

"Will they restore things [at will and by themselves]? Will they [try to bribe their God] with sacrifice?" Please be aware that your adversary will continually mock and ridicule the working of the Lord in and around the kingdom of heaven in your life. The kingdom of heaven has always, and will always, be opposed in our lives. We need to judge the way the Lord sees things, not necessarily going the way we think things should go.

The Enemy Uses Multiple Tactics

> But when Sanballat, Tobiah, the Arabians, Ammonites, and Ashdodites heard that the walls of Jerusalem were going up and that the breaches were being closed, they were very angry. [8]And they all plotted together to come and fight against Jerusalem, to injure and cause confusion and failure in it.[10]And [the leaders of] Judah said, The strength of the burden bearers is weakening, and

there is much rubbish; we are not able to work on the wall. ¹¹And our enemies said, They will not know or see till we come into their midst and kill them and stop the work. (Nehemiah 10:7–11)

Has anyone ever been mad at you because of the mandate you carry? They may not say it, but you can tell they are really angry and bothered because you are not focused on their issues. The enemy does not like it when people have a mandate. Do not back down and or be distracted in your pursuit of the Lord. If people oppose Christianity or an increase of the Lord operating in their lives, they are for sure going to oppose you getting closer to God. We need to understand this opposition and say, "I am going to be opposed, but I am choosing to walk with the Lord."

There are patterns you need to understand. There are mounds of rubbish in the world that come to discourage you in the pursuit of the Lord. Understand that we do not wrestle against flesh and blood; therefore, no person is ever your enemy. Opposition simply manifests through people's lives, much like Godly revelation manifests through our lives. Different tactics are used—like ridicule, mockery, and anger. *"Sanballat and Geshem sent to me, saying, Come, let us meet together in one of the villages in the plain of Ono. But they intended to do me harm"* (Nehemiah 6:2). If the enemy can't do something, he will hire someone else to do it.

I went into the house of Shemaiah son of Delaiah, the son of Mehetabel, who was shut up. He said, Let us meet together in the house of God, within the temple, and let us shut the doors of the temple, for they are coming to kill you—at night they are coming to kill you. ¹¹But I said, Should such a man as I flee? And what man such as I could go into the temple [where only the priests are allowed to go] and yet live? I will not go in.¹²And behold, I saw that God had not sent him, but he made this prophecy against me because Tobiah and Sanballat had hired him. ¹³He was hired that I should be made afraid and do as he said and sin, that they might have matter for an evil report with which to taunt and reproach me.¹⁴My God, think on Tobiah and Sanballat according to these their works, and on the prophetess Noadiah and the rest of the prophets who would have put me in fear.¹⁵So the wall was finished on the twenty-fifth day of the month Elul, in fifty-two days.¹⁶When all our enemies heard of it, all the nations around us feared and fell far in their own esteem, for they saw that this work was done by our God. ¹⁷Moreover, in those days the nobles of Judah sent many letters to Tobiah, and Tobiah's letters came to them.¹⁸For many in Judah were bound by oath to him, because he was the son-in-law of Shecaniah son of Arah, and his son Jehohanan had married the daughter of Meshullam son of Berechiah.¹⁹Also they spoke of [Tobiah's] good deeds before me and told him what I said. And Tobiah sent letters to frighten me. (Nehemiah 6:10–19)

In the scripture, the situation is starting to escalate. Nehemiah is told by his friend, *"They are coming to kill you."* There is one that has been killed for us. If you declare the mandate of heaven, you will have opposition. There is no such thing as "nice Christianese." You are in a war, whether you like it or not. If the enemy can't get you in one area, he will try another way. He uses multiple tactics. Remember that it is okay to dream. When the dream is from God, it will be opposed. The Lord is the only one who can make it happen. He is the master builder.

CHAPTER SIXTEEN

Total and Complete Surrender to Him

Live Each Day as Though It Were Your Last

> Now may the God of peace who brought up our Lord
> Jesus from the dead, that great Shepherd of the sheep,
> through the blood of the everlasting covenant, [21]make
> you complete in every good work to do His will, work-
> ing in you what is well pleasing in His sight, through
> Jesus Christ, to whom be glory forever and ever. Amen.
> (Hebrews 13:20–21, NKJV)

Christian life should be exciting. If being a Christian is not exciting,
something needs to change. We need to surrender every day. Surrendering means yielding ownership and laying down control of our

lives. There are no exceptions. The scripture says, *"Then He said to them all, 'If anyone desires to come after Me, let him deny himself, and take up his cross daily, and follow Me'"* (Luke 9:23, NKJV). The Lord is always at work, even when we don't understand it. We need to stay obedient to His Word.

I have had a chance to pray over many people who have overdosed on drugs. They took too many drugs, for many different reasons, and they had no relationship with the Lord. They have all been healed in the name of Jesus. I asked each one of them the same questions. I asked, "If you knew where you would be today, would you have changed anything?" I want to ask you the same question. Even though we all know that someday we are going to die, do we live with that reality in our mind? Do we consider it when we make our daily choices? We need to be asking the Lord how He wants us to live every single day.

Each and every person is called to make a difference in this world. We need to establish in ourselves lifestyles of surrender. Jesus went to the cross. His mind was struggling with control. He prayed to His Father, *"O My Father, if it is possible, let this cup pass from Me; nevertheless, not as I will, but as You will"* (Matthew 26:39, NKJV). The strategy of heaven is to see the kingdom of God go forth. In order to do this, we need to completely surrender, giving up and laying everything down. Surrender is a lifestyle that the Lord endorses. We need to live for Christ as though it is our last day. This is my challenge to you—live each and every day as though it was your last day to see the kingdom of God advance on earth.

One day I found myself at the gym having a conversation with a young man. He asked me, "Is my life really making a difference in this world?"

I said to him, "If you are living a lifestyle of surrender, you are always making a difference."

Christianity has had a "What's in it for me?" mentality for too long. There is unnecessary sin in our lives which causes suffering. Sin is the only form of suffering that a Christian can control. This gentleman at the gym was basically asking me, "Is my life pleasing to the Lord?" I want to ask you the same question. Is your life pleasing to the Lord today? This may challenge you. It challenges me daily. The Lord is asking us to walk in a realm of glory by His Spirit. It can't be done in your own strength. You can be enabled and equipped to walk the way He desires for your life through the power of the Holy Spirit, and you can live Godly with an open heaven surrounding your life.

Walk in Weakness

A surrendered lifestyle will always make a difference. *"I have been crucified with Christ; it is no longer I who live, but Christ lives in me; and the life which I now live in the flesh I live by faith in the Son of God, who loved me and gave Himself for me"* (Galatians 2:20, NKJV). A surrendered lifestyle looks like Christ. What is motivating your life? Is it finances, relationships, ambition, or where you think you should be? You need to be motivated by Christ. Everyone wants to go to heaven, but no one wants to die. The Bible says, *"I affirm, by the boasting in you which I have in Christ Jesus our Lord, I die daily"* (1 Corinthians 15:31, NKJV). Our focus should not be to appear strong. Instead of manifesting our strengths, the Lord is calling us to walk in our weaknesses. In the Bible, the Lord says, *"My grace is sufficient for you, for My strength is made perfect in weakness"* (2 Corinthians 12:9, NKJV). Do not be afraid of weakness. Weakness is, in fact, strength for you. Many of us subconsciously do things in our own strength by drawing upon our own resources. In our weakness, we are able to draw into the strength of the Lord so that we will know He is the one who is achieving it through us.

Please Him in All Things

> I appeal to you therefore, brethren, and beg of you in view of [all] the mercies of God, to make a decisive dedication of your bodies [presenting all your members and faculties] as a living sacrifice, holy (devoted, consecrated) and well pleasing to God, which is your reasonable (rational, intelligent) service and spiritual worship. (Roman's 12:1)

This scripture is saying, "Hey I beg you, I appeal to you. Hear by the Spirit." You need to become a living sacrifice. This may involve laying things down that control your life. For some reason, we have a hard time dying to things that prevent us from experiencing more of Him.

> Therefore, whether we are at home [on earth away from Him] or away from home [and with Him], we are constantly ambitious and strive earnestly to be pleasing to Him. (2 Corinthians 5:9)

In your life are you striving to be *"earnestly pleasing to Him"*? Are you striving in your life to be pleasing to God?

> That you may walk (live and conduct yourselves) in a manner worthy of the Lord, fully pleasing to Him and desiring to please Him in all things, bearing fruit in

every good work and steadily growing and increasing in and by the knowledge of God [with fuller, deeper, and clearer insight, acquaintance, and recognition]. (Colossians 1:10)

We need to desire to please Him in all things. Every day we can go higher than the day before. I don't believe in going backwards or treading water. In the church I pastor, we don't have reverse or neutral. We only have forward gears. You can't look at your inability. He is completely able. The Lord only does good work; therefore, you are a good work.

Now may the God of peace who brought up our Lord Jesus from the dead, that great Shepherd of the sheep, through the blood of the everlasting covenant, 21make you complete in every good work to do His will, working in you what is well pleasing in His sight, through Jesus Christ, to whom be glory forever and ever. Amen. (Hebrews 13:20–21, NKJV)

And whatever we ask we receive from Him, because we keep His commandments and do those things that are pleasing in His sight. (1 John 3:22, NKJV)

Not that I have already attained, or am already perfected; but I press on, that I may lay hold of that for which Christ Jesus has also laid hold of me. 13Brethren, I do not count myself to have apprehended; but one thing I do, forgetting those things which are behind and reaching forward to those things which are ahead, [14]I press toward the goal for the prize of the upward call of God in Christ Jesus. (Philippians 3:12–14, NKJV)

Jesus is laying hold of you today. You need to forget any past mistakes that you have made. It is time to move forward in a lifestyle of surrender that has been released through Him. With the Lord, you can't make a mistake. The Bible says, *"All things work together for good to those who love God, to those who are the called according to His purpose"* (Romans 8:28, NKJV). Stop minimizing God in your life and focusing on your inabilities. The Lord uses what we may consider mistakes to massage our lives. Christ moulds us through surrender.

My grace is sufficient for you, for My strength is made perfect in weakness. (2 Corinthians 12:9, NKJV).

CHAPTER SEVENTEEN

We Were Made for Him

Allow the Holy Spirit to Put You Over

You were made for the Lord Jesus—not anyone else. You were created for complete communion with Him. I believe that we should be examining our hearts daily. The Bible says, *"The heart is deceitful above all things, and desperately wicked; who can know it?"* (Jeremiah 17:9, NKJV) Unless our heart is regenerated by the Spirit of the Lord, it is deceitful. One of my challenges every day is getting close to the Lord and letting Him examine my heart. I want Him to change me from the inside out. We need to love the Lord totally and completely. He loves us totally and completely. He wants to transform us, but regardless, He still loves us. The Lord does not desire for anything that happens to us to be wasted. He wants us to use it to draw closer to Him. Without the

Lord, we have nothing. I hunger and thirst for more of Him daily. I can't do anything without Him. I can't string a sentence together but by the power of the Holy Spirit.

Most Christians wallow at such a low level. We should definitely be living more abundantly. Why are Christians just getting enough to survive when the Lord has made a breakthrough for us? Why is it that so much goes on around us? Why is it that we are being attacked constantly? I believe that it has a lot to do with position. We are called to be positioned in the heavenly realm far above principalities, rulers, and dominions. In essence we should have a realm of heaven functioning in our lives. This realm is not for the sweet by and by.

I am not minimizing the fact that Christians have to go through a lot. Most of Christianity is under burdens or weights. The challenge is to not allow weights from the enemy to put you under, but to allow the Holy Spirit to put you over. *"We are more than conquerors through Him who loved us"* (Romans 8:37, NKJV). The reality of the Gospel is that he *"raised us up together, and made us sit together in the heavenly places in Christ Jesus"* (Ephesians 2:6, NKJV).

The Lord Is Fine Tuning Us

When you get a new guitar, the first thing you need to do is tune it. When you drive your car and it is chugging along, you get a tune-up. This is similar to what the Lord is doing with us. He is preparing and fine-tuning us. We need to declare a breakthrough in our lives. It is not about what you can do; it is about what He can do. I received a vision from the Lord of a new banqueting table one morning during prayer. I believe there is a new banqueting table available to us.

Many people have put prayers in dormancy. I believe we are entering a season of unprecedented answers to prayer. We can be positioned to make declarations into the atmosphere. When we decree something, we will see it established. This is what it means to manifest heaven on earth. The Lord wants to restore those unanswered prayers in your life. If you have dropped answers to prayer, it is time to put it on the front burner. Do not lay down prophesies that have been given to you in the past and were confirmed in your life. If you thirst and hunger for the Lord, things will become very clear in your life. The Lord desires for you to walk a purposeful life. When you are a threat to the enemy, you may come under attack. It is time for the enemy to be intimidated. Christians are not wimpy, because Christ was not a wimp; therefore, you are not a wimp.

Wherever the Lord Jesus went, principalities and demons would start to manifest. The protection of the Lord was upon Him completely. It did not leave Him. Jesus was able to fulfill the destiny on His life. We are called to stir things up by the Spirit of the Lord, but certainly not outside of the Lord's doing. Do not be afraid of the devil. When I walk into a restaurant and hear people swearing, I just smile and start saying, "Praise the Lord. Hallelujah!" Please understand that the devil is afraid of you walking in God's authority. It is time for the enemy to become intimidated by what you carry, not the other way around. It is time for the enemy to be on the run. Don't let this opportunity pass you by. You can walk with a heavenly authority in your life.

Don't Fear the Fire

One Friday morning during prayer time, we were having communion, which we do daily. I heard a mighty wind begin to blow by the Spirit. I felt the Lord say, "Get ready for the wind of the Spirit to blow over your life. A fresh new wind of the Lord is available. I am not holding back." I want this wind now, and so should you. When you intimidate the devil, do not be surprised when he counterattacks.

Another morning during prayer, I felt the Lord show me that the enemy was working on an attack. All of a sudden, a story came on Facebook about Frontline Worship Centre, the church I pastor. Someone had posted on Facebook that "Frontline Worship centre is the most evil and vile church out there." This completely confirmed what the Lord had shown me just a few short days earlier. It also told me that our church was headed in the right direction. Do not be afraid of persecution. Jesus was opposed. Most of the apostles were murdered. Understand that persecution usually means you are doing something right, unless of course you are walking in sin. Don't back down. Don't be afraid of the fire. Fire refines.

I have been a believer for thirty-six years. Every day I look at scripture in a fresh new way. I must continually challenge my heart to see all scripture with a heart of revelation. Do not let fear prevent you from entering into the Lord's presence. There are new mysteries and secrets of the kingdom of God being released. Don't miss out on what He desires to share with you. It is time to get out of the emotional realm of the soul, which will always limit the Lord.

There were two trees in the Garden—one was the Tree of Life, and the other was the Tree of Knowledge of Good and Evil. You don't want the evil one. Get out of your emotions. They are controlled by your soul man. Adam and Eve fell because of issues of the soul, and it is this very strategy that limits mankind and heaven manifesting in your life. Allow your Spirit man to be in control.

Someone once said to me, "The Lord gave us emotions and a mind." This is a true enough statement. What I don't believe is that our emotions and mind were the same before the fall of humanity in the Garden. In other words, our state of being was much different before the fall. When sin entered humanity, our emotions and state of mind became something much different than before the fall. When Adam and Eve walked with God, there was only one truth—the truth of God. After the fall, something shifted in us and totally changed our perceptions on things. This is why we need to have the mind of Christ, to release a manifested heaven on earth. In the Garden, our emotions and mind were not the same as what we have today. In the Garden, we were totally influenced by God. He was the only truth. Then the fall of man took place. It wasn't God's word anymore; it was, "Mmm, that looks good." Understand that there are Godly emotions. It was very different before the fall of man than it is today.

What Are You Built On?

According to the grace (the special endowment for my task) of God bestowed on me, like a skilful architect and master builder I laid [the] foundation, and now another [man] is building upon it. But let each [man] be careful how he builds upon it, for no other foundation can anyone lay than that which is [already] laid, which is Jesus Christ (the Messiah, the Anointed One). But if anyone builds upon the Foundation, whether it be with gold, silver, precious stones, wood, hay, straw, the work of each [one] will become [plainly, openly] known (shown for

what it is); for the day [of Christ] will disclose and declare it, because it will be revealed with fire, and the fire
will test and critically appraise the character and worth
of the work each person has done. If the work which
any person has built on this Foundation [any product
of his efforts whatever] survives [this test], he will get
his reward. But if any person's work is burned up [under
the test], he will suffer the loss [of it all, losing his re-
ward], though he himself will be saved, but only as [one
who has passed] through fire. Do you not discern and
understand that you [the whole church at Corinth] are
God's temple (His sanctuary), and that God's Spirit has
His permanent dwelling in you [to be at home in you,
collectively as a church and also individually]? If anyone
does hurt to God's temple or corrupts it [with false doc-
trines] or destroys it, God will do hurt to him and bring
him to the corruption of death and destroy him. For the
temple of God is holy (sacred to Him) and that [temple]
you [the believing church and its individual believers]
are. (1 Corinthians 3:10–17)

In this scripture, Paul is speaking about the church. I, however, am
applying it to our individual hearts. *"According to the grace (the special endowment for my task) of God bestowed on me..."* We need to believe and know that God's grace is planted in our hearts. His grace is
always available. It is there to fulfill the destiny the Lord has for our
lives. We can't do it but, the Lord can. *"...like a skilful architect and
master builder..."* With the grace of God, we need to build ourselves.

This can be done by positioning ourselves and changing our mindsets. For example, the poverty mindset—you may be rich and still feel poor. *"...I laid [the] foundation, and now another [man] is building upon it."* Specific mindsets affect the structure of the building. For example, fear. Fear of death or the future influence us at times over our faith. No one is exempt from it. The problem is that people do things out of fear and claim it to be faith. The Lord moves through faith. Everything that you receive from the Lord will be tested. Many times it is the Lord who is testing you.

"But let each [man] be careful how he builds upon it..." Be careful about what you are building upon. Is it fear or faith? What is your foundation? Is it sand or rock? Are you walking around with fear and torment? Is your foundation built on critiquing everything or being critical, or is built on love and acceptance? *"...for no other foundation can anyone lay than that which is [already] laid, which is Jesus Christ (the Messiah, the Anointed One)."* This is what we need—the Lord Jesus Christ. He is the only thing we should be looking for. Everything else will get you off-track. You need to be built on Him. Everything else is garbage.

"But if anyone builds upon the Foundation, whether it be with gold, silver, precious stones, wood, hay, straw, the work of each [one] will become [plainly, openly] known." The test is time. In time, everyone's work will become plainly and openly known. Your relationship with the Lord needs to be built on rock—not shifting sand. You can purpose this for this today. Then in five, ten, or twenty years, no storm can take you out. You will be able to say, "No I am built on the rock of the Lord Jesus Christ." If you don't believe it, start declaring it over your life every day. Declare, "He is my foundation, high tower, refuge, and peace." When

you declare things in the spiritual realm, you achieve spiritual results. I am built on the rock of the Lord Jesus Christ. What are you declaring over yourself and your family? Circumstances lie. You need to declare the truth: "I am built on the rock."

"For the day [of Christ] will disclose and declare it..." Your foundation is the most important thing. That foundation can shift when you make small adjustments to what you believe. Some churches are dead because the Spirit of the Lord has stopped functioning within them. The reason is because they shifted their foundation. They started saying, "Maybe we will shift a tiny bit so more people come to our church." I am not opposed to churches and church growth, but be careful what you are building upon. Love people, but don't condone sin. *"...because it will be revealed with fire, and the fire will test and critically appraise the character and worth of the work each person has done."* The fire is coming. If you are not built on rock, fire will burn you. We will all be tested. What is your foundation built upon? If it is rock, the fire will not burn you. If you build on the right foundation, the scripture says, *"He will get his reward."* This is a byproduct for going after Jesus and heaven in your life. If you are proposing to do something that does not line up with the Word of God, it is wrong. Our emotions should not dictate an ungodly response to anything.

> Until his word [to his cruel brothers] came true, until the
> word of the Lord tried and tested him. (Psalms 105:19)

This is David speaking about Joseph. Joseph endured a lot. He was in the pit, and then out of the pit. He was going to be killed, and then not going to be killed. He was sold to slavery, put in jail, and falsely accused. Satan is *"the accuser of [the] brethren"* (Revelation 12:10, NKJV).

The Word of the Lord tested him. The Word of the Lord will also test you. Do not be afraid to be tested by the Lord. Do not mistake it for the devil. When the Lord tests you, good comes out of it.

CHAPTER EIGHTEEN

What Really Happened in the Garden of Eden?

What Did Adam Do?

Something happened in the Garden of Eden that changed humanity. Sometimes I think, *I'd like to have a real good talk with Adam.* Why did he allow such a thing to happen when he had received the Word of the Lord? He really was at the centre of this change. Christianity doesn't like to talk about what really happened in the Garden.

> And it was not Adam who was deceived, but [the] woman who was deceived and deluded and fell into transgression. (1 Timothy 2:14)

The first eight words of this scripture changed the course of humanity. *"And it was not Adam who was deceived."* If Adam wasn't deceived, then what did he do? He did something that changed the course of humanity. Something happened in the Garden that allowed us to be deceived. According to the Bible, Adam wasn't deceived. Whatever it was that happened plagued humanity for thousands of years and continues to do so. When the Lord showed me this, I wept inside. Man consciously put something above God. Man knew the truth because God had spoken the truth. *"The Truth will set you free"* (John 8:32). Everything else blinds you. The truth brings freedom. Humanity has dealt with this over and over.

I specifically want to focus on the reality of what Adam did. I am not concerned about Eve, although her deception is a matter of human history with God. If Adam was not deceived, then what happened with him? *"The Lord God commanded the man, saying, You may freely eat of every tree of the garden; But of the tree of the knowledge of good and evil and blessing and calamity you shall not eat, for in the day that you eat of it you shall surely die"* (Genesis 2:16–17). God spoke to Adam in the form of a commandment. This was the very first commandment for all life to flow.

Something Attractive that Will Lead to Death

I was raised in a city. Sometimes we would go out to the country to my mom's family's farm. They had fly paper. This paper would attract flies and the very thing that attracted the flies to the paper was what killed them. They were attracted to something that would ultimately kill them. The same thing happens with mosquito zappers that hang outside. Mosquitos beeline to the zapper and it kills them.

In Africa, malaria is widespread, a disease that spreads through mosquito bites. When I was there, I was being bit by mosquitos all over the place. All of a sudden, people I was with brought out something that resembled a tennis racquet. It was a bug zapper. I said, "Where has this bug zapper been for the last ten days while I was being bitten like crazy?"

The reality is that something is out there that attracts humanity that will result in our death, and it is part of our natural human nature. Addicts know, for the most part, that they are going to die. They have an attraction even though they know it leads to death. All of us struggle with a form of weakness or temptation. If you say you don't, you are lying. I know, because Jesus was tempted in all things. There are weaknesses in humanity. Mine might not be the same as yours, but we all have a spirit trapped in our human bodies. We all have one. I have been trying to process this.

Think about Samson. Samson was called to be a Nazerite. In the Bible, it is written, *"The vow of a Nazirite, that is, one separated and consecrated to the Lord"* (Numbers 6:2). An angel of the Lord came to Samson's mother and said, *"No razor shall come upon his head, for the child shall be a Nazirite to God from birth"* (Judges 13:5). He was a strong man with one weakness, "no razor shall come upon his head." He could not cut his hair. The Philistines were terrified of him. What attracted Samson to Delilah in the Bible? Delilah is thought of as someone with an hourglass figure. Let me say this—It wasn't sex that attracted Samson to Delilah.

Delilah was chosen of the enemy to find out Samson's secret. Anointed people have a secret strength. You may be an anointed worshiper, intercessor, or preacher of the Gospel; the devil doesn't want you to operate in your anointing. He will use everything to disarm your strength. Samson knew exactly what Delilah was doing. He knew he was playing with fire. Samson lied to Delilah four times before he told her the truth. If he had full trust in her, he wouldn't have lied. He knew she was out to kill him. We need to understand that not everyone who comes into our lives is with us or for us. The battle is not between flesh and blood. The wrestle is against principalities, powers, and rulers of darkness in high places. The enemy will use people to try and find out your strength. He wants you out of the race. He wants to "cut your hair." I am not giving up my strength for anything, and I refuse to place myself into a position where this may occur.

Samson knew Delilah was not for him. She was against him, and being used by the enemy. He thought he was strong and he put too much trust in his own strength, much like we do from time to time. He had terrorized the Philistines and taken up the gates. They were afraid of him. The devil is afraid of you and me. If Samson was aware of Delilah's motives, why was he drawn to her? Virtually for the same reason flies are attracted to fly paper. She wanted to destroy him. In the Garden, Adam knew that he was drawn to something that would destroy him. Throughout Christian history, the enemy has tried to destroy us. He sends people on assignment to find our strength and "cut our hair." We need to be aware that something inside of us inherently wants to choose death. Adam and Samson made conscious decisions that they knew would ultimately lead to death. There are many others who did the same thing throughout history.

Making these decisions will do one of two things; it will abort the plan of God or put it off for a season, preventing heaven from manifesting in your life. It could be any weakness—it could be sex, anger, or a critical spirit. People who do not hold your best interest will try and fuel your weakness. Misery loves company. If you struggle with something in your life, you will draw people to you who have that same struggle. The enemy uses these people to get each other off-track. Understand that we all have strength, but at the same time we all have weakness. If you think you are strong, the enemy has direct access. This is what happened to Samson.

> And she said to him, How can you say, I love you, when your heart is not with me? You have mocked me these three times and have not told me in what your great strength lies. (Judges 16: 15)

"You have mocked me these three times." Delilah asked Samson three times where his great strength lay. She was on assignment. There is an assignment against you. Whatever dangerous behaviour you participate in is trying to draw you away from God. It could be speeding, not wearing your seatbelt, texting while driving, or skydiving without a parachute.

Guard Your Life

> With such nagging she prodded him day after day until he was tired to death. So he told her everything. "No razor has ever been used on my head," he said, "because I have been a Nazirite set apart to God since birth. If my head were shaved, my strength would leave me, and I would become as weak as any other man." When Delilah saw that he had told her everything, she sent word to the rulers of the Philistines, "Come back once more; he has told me everything." So the rulers of the

Philistines returned with the silver in their hands. Having put him to sleep on her lap, she called a man to shave off the seven braids of his hair, and so began to subdue him. And his strength left him. Then she called, "Samson, the Philistines are upon you!" He awoke from his sleep and thought, "I'll go out as before and shake myself free." But he did not know that the Lord had left him. Then the Philistines seized him, gouged out his eyes and took him down to Gaza. Binding him with bronze shackles, they set him to grinding in the prison. (Judges 16:16–21, NIV)

Samson was tired! He told Delilah everything she wanted to know because he was weary and tired. Samson did this because he was worn down and weary. Weary means that he had lost pleasure in what he was doing. Have you ever been prone to do something when you were weary that you wouldn't have done otherwise? The devil will do whatever it takes to rob you of your strength. The higher you go with the Lord, the greater the opposition. You need to guard your life. The mandate of heaven is on your life. Don't take this lightly. You are here on earth to achieve what the Lord desires for you to achieve. In my career as an RCMP officer, I could have been killed four or five times. I know that I am here for such a time as this. The reality is that we are all on earth to advance the kingdom of God and see heaven manifest. Guarding our hearts needs to be a priority.

The Enemy Will Take Your Strength and Sight

"So the rulers of the Philistines returned with the silver in their hands. Having put him to sleep on her lap..." Samson was tired and sleeping on Delilah's lap. If you are married, you would assume this was a safe place to nap. Your house should be a safe place of refuge for your spouse, a place they can go to get strong in the Lord. *"...she called a man to shave off the seven braids of his hair..."* Samson slept in the lap of the woman he loved and trusted, knowing she wanted to destroy him. He slept through his hair being cut. Has anyone slept through a haircut at a barber shop? *"And his strength left him. Then she called, 'Samson, the Philistines are upon you!'"* She called him because she wanted to see if he still had strength. *"[Samson] thought, 'I'll go out as before and shake myself free.' But he did not know that the Lord had left him."*

When you lose your strength, you don't know it is gone. You think you are the same as before. You think you still have the anointing the Lord gave you. When it's too late, you find out that it is gone in a time of overwhelming need. *"Then the Philistines seized him, gouged out his eyes and took him down to Gaza."* After he lost his strength, they took his sight. He was blind. When you give your strength to a known adversary, the devil desires to take your spiritual sight. You think you have your strength, but it is gone. You think you have your sight, but it is gone. This all happened because you chose something that you knew would lead to death. After this all happened to Samson, they bound *him "with bronze shackles, they set him to grinding in the prison."* He was a prisoner again. Jesus came to set us free and give us life. The enemy came to rob, kill, and destroy. You need your strength and your sight for your breakthrough and victory. Do not let the enemy achieve his goal of taking your strength, and therefore your spiritual sight.

The Lord Desires to Restore Sight

> I had heard of You [only] by the hearing of the ear, but
> now my [spiritual] eye sees You. (Job 42: 5)

Job went through a lot. He lost family, fortune, and basically everything. Through this, something was established. His adversary was the devil. *"My [spiritual] eye sees you."* You can have eyes to see the Lord. If the enemy has taken your strength or sight, I believe the Lord desires to restore it. One of the greatest miracles that are performed time and time again is the return of sight. It is available to you.

CHAPTER NINETEEN

Surrendered to the Will of Another

If you want more of the power of God and His manifested heaven in your life, you must know that it comes out of a flow of surrendering yourself to the Lord. No one has arrived completely, but He is looking for obedient hearts. In prayer, we focus on the Lord and His presence, but the key is to let the Lord deal with our hearts first.

Everyone has been wounded, including Jesus Himself, who was wounded on our behalf. Years ago, someone approached me and said, "Pastor, I think you're wounded." I thought about it for a quarter of a second. In my heart, I thought, "You think?" If you are wounded and need deliverance, it is important to arrange to receive that. There is something in surrendering everything to the Lord that releases the power of the Holy Spirit.

There is a reality and understanding that I desire to impart to the universal church. The presence of the Lord changes everything in your life. What is lacking in your life? Yes, you are going to be wounded. You will have suffering, perhaps struggling financially or with relationships, but there is a higher reality that flows out of the presence of God. The Lord changes everything. You cannot change yourself. In the presence of God, everything can be changed or turned around in a single second under His presence. When I am asked to counsel people, I am always up for it. I end up repeating the things that I have said in my sermons. Oh that we would have ears to hear and eyes to see by the Holy Spirit.

Jesus didn't want to give up His life. He said, *"Nevertheless, not as I will, but as You"* (Matthew 26:39, NKJV). Now is a great time to tap into the will of God. Let me be clear that our understandings may be very different. I am declaring into the spiritual atmosphere that you are more than conquerors in Christ. The Lord is the author and finisher of my faith. He is not finished with us yet. He looks at us as a work in progress from beginning to end, if you allow Him to do so.

Last year, there were three or four areas in which the Lord asked me to surrender. I surrendered the church I pastor. I am not averse to doing those things, because I am after the heart of the Lord, His desires, and what He wants to see for each and every one of us. It comes from a flow of the presence of God. I weep at what people go through. I hate seeing people go through hurtful things; I hurt because the Lord hurts, and He grieves over our situations.

> He released the man who had been thrown into prison for insurrection and murder, the one they asked for, and surrendered Jesus to their will. (Luke 23:25, NIV)

I have meditated on the last five words in this verse for an extended period of time. The reality is that we need to be dead within ourselves. We need to be dead and have our lives submitted and surrendered not only to the Lord but to others as well. The words *submit* and *surrender* mean the same thing in the scriptures, and if you want more of God, that is what you need to do. We need to be purposefully submitted and surrendered first and foremost to the Lord, and then to others. Somehow we think the people in the Bible are different from us in the sense that they can achieve miraculous things of the Lord. Really, they were people the same as we are. They had keys and understanding empowered by the Spirit of the Lord. It is like the tip of an iceberg. We are only on the tip, but there are so many mysteries and secrets to be revealed in our lives to see His manifestation unfold for us.

You may be happy with your life and not want to go any further. Jesus submitted himself totally and completely to others. It is a biblical principal. Most Christians agree when it comes to surrendering themselves to one another. The power, anointing, and grace of God is released out of a heart of surrender. Maybe this isn't for you, but maybe it is. I believe that the anointing we saw in the days of old is available for us when we line up under a manifested heaven. It is not the "same old, same old." That won't cut it anymore. It is not about who did what over there and why and analyzing everything that happens. It is about your heart and surrendering yourself to Him. You have no rights. In police terminology in Canada, there is a statement police officers must read to suspects and it goes like this: "You have the right to remain silent. Anything you say can and will be used in a court of law."

The first detachment I was posted to out of police training was in Outlook, Saskatchewan. This was where I met my beautiful wife Cathryn. The rule of the day was that if you decided as a bachelor to marry someone from the local area, you would be immediately transferred to another location to avoid any favouritism being extended to the in-laws, so to speech. As a result of this rule, when I announced my engagement to Cathryn it was decided that I would be relocated to a detachment a considerable distance away. They probably felt I would have a hard time giving my wife a ticket for speeding, for example.

On my last night in Outlook, the detachment had a going away party for me at the residence of one of my co-workers. It happened to be a block and a half away from the detachment office. There was no one doing police work in that sixty-mile radius surrounding the detachment, as everyone was at my going away party. If a serious call would have come in, the neighbouring detachment was to handle it. They would respond to anything serious. This practise, I believe, still continues today because resources are so thin.

As is my custom, I was the first to leave the party. When I went outside, I saw an individual sitting in the front seat of my brother-in-law's pickup truck behind the steering wheel. He was bent over, trying to hotwire the vehicle. The funny thing was that the keys were sitting on top of the dash! I walked up to the window and said, "Hey buddy, what are you doing?" He concocted a rather lengthy and not at all convincing story about how he had lost his keys. He happened to know a thing or two about getting his vehicle hotwired. I was thanking God that I had the opportunity to see this happen. Out of all the vehicles within a sixty-mile radius, this guy attempted to steal a vehicle at my going away party when there were no police officers working. I then told the guy he was under arrest for attempting to steal a motor vehicle. I showed him my badge and informed him that he was trying to steal a vehicle in front of a party full of police officers. This gentleman fought and kicked and screamed all the one and a half blocks back to the detachment cells. It wasn't particularly the height of a surrendered lifestyle.

> But whatever were gains to me I now consider loss for the sake of Christ. [8]What is more, I consider everything a loss because of the surpassing worth of knowing Christ Jesus my Lord, for whose sake I have lost all things. I consider them garbage, that I may gain Christ [9]and be found in him, not having a righteousness of my own that comes from the law, but that which is through faith in Christ—the righteousness that comes from God on the basis of faith. [10]I want to know Christ—yes, to know the power of his resurrection and participation in his sufferings, becoming like him in his death, [11]and so, somehow, attaining to the resurrection from the dead. [12]Not that I have already obtained all this, or have already arrived at my goal, but I press on to take hold of that for which Christ Jesus took hold of me. (Philippians 3: 7–12, NIV)

"Not having a righteousness of my own..." We are all garbage and dirt in the natural. We were created out of dirt, and we will eventually return to dirt, at least apart from the spirit portion of ourselves. There is an element within all of us that will continue to live on after our natural death. Christ has taken a hold of you. He chose you before you chose

him. He saw you before you were in your mother's womb. He knows you better than you know yourself.

> You haven't come to a blast from God's trumpet. You haven't come to a voice speaking to you. When people heard that voice long ago, they begged it not to say anything more to them. (Hebrews 12:9, NIV)

The Gospel is opposite of the natural in the sense that we want to hold on to our lives and try and keep them. We seem to want things a certain way. If you want life, you need to surrender it. That is a spiritual reality. Give your life up so that you can receive His life. These spiritual principles need to be applied to your life. You can be stubborn as an ox and still be saved and go to heaven, but a surrendered lifestyle will produce a manifested heaven in your life on earth. It quite literally is Christ living through you!

> Submit to God. Stand up to the devil. He will run away from you. (James 4:7, NIV)

Surrender yourself to God. Just die to your way of doing things. You can still be attacked and wounded. Surrendering yourself is not a very popular topic, particularly in this modern age we find ourselves in. Everyone ever used of God first had to surrender their will to the will of God, and out of that flow they were able to walk in a realm of the supernatural under a manifested heaven. I realize that surrendering your life is not an easy thing to do. It was not easy for the Lord to lay His will down in the Garden of Gethsemane, but He clearly did so for the prize He saw before Him. What prize does the Lord have before you? I believe Christ achieved something very special for us—you are not only going to heaven, but you can expect to walk in a realm of His glory here on earth, irrespective of circumstances. He is resident in your life and He will make all the difference!

CHAPTER TWENTY

The Fundamental Error and the Stand of Love

The topic in this chapter is something that many do not desire to embrace. In many cases, I see a very self-serving form of the Gospel being advanced when our focus ought to be on the advancement of Christ-centeredness and the kingdom of God. I believe this is changing in this day and hour as we enter into the age of the perfecting of the Bride of Christ, which ushers in a manifested heaven upon this earth. If you catch what is being discussed here by the Spirit of the Lord, you will have a great foundation for a manifested heaven in your life.

The role of the fivefold ministry is to equip the saints until we come into the fullness of the Lord Jesus Christ. The presence of the Lord, interestingly enough, is not rooted in religious form, ritual, or tradition, but rather it is rooted in a relationship with the Lord Jesus

Christ—a relationship that must be careful preserved, nurtured, and sustained to see growth, if indeed we are after growth. A religious walk is full of rules, regulations, and bondage, along with an "I will hold you under until you submit" attitude. The mandate of the universal church is the presence of the Lord. In the presence of the Lord, everything in your life will change as you become transformed from the inside out—not the other way around. In other words, it won't happen from the outside in.

One morning in our morning prayer service, the Lord dropped on my heart the thought that He wants us all to come against religious mindsets. This is, indeed, not a popular topic, but nevertheless it's an incredibly important one to have heaven manifest in your life. Come against traditional religious mindsets that prevent the manifested presence of God for your life. Let's be clear: everyone wrestles against mindsets that are not consistent with the mind of Christ.

My computer crashed on me one day recently, and when my assistant took it to the computer technician, his words were, "All the data is there, but you just can't access it." The computer would turn on, but then loop back to the process of turning on again and again without entering into the fullness of what it was intended for. I describe this loop as a "fundamental error." When there is a fundamental error, the data may be there but you can't access or get at it.

Now, I would like to take this general computer principle and apply it to a spiritual reality. All the attributes of Christianity may be in your life, but because you can't get through this fundamental error, you don't have access to the mysteries and secrets the Lord desires to release in this hour. Believe me, they are available to you once you take His dominion and authority to resolve any fundamental error. If you are not experienced in religious circles, you may not understand that this fundamental loop concept goes on all the time in many individuals' lives. This very thing that causes many not to have eyes to see nor ears to hear clearly by the Spirit in this season of time. Religion tries to invade us, but we do not want any part of it, nor should we have any part of it. So within this context, we come against a fundamental error which prevents us from experiencing a manifested heaven in our lives. This error quite literally prevents us from coming into the full manifestation of the Gospel, which has been released for those who believe.

I am not opposed to taking down mindsets, nor should you be, and an examination of why we do things the way we do should be a daily event to determine if they are consistent with Him. Everywhere Jesus went, He took down religious mindsets and challenged those around Him to do the same thing. In part, I believe that this aspect is very important for the modern-day Christian living out their belief in a world opposed to this belief. I feel privileged to be a part of taking down religious mindsets, starting with my own. Having said that, don't be surprised if there is turmoil against it. If you open your heart and let the Lord do the work, you are going to have access to so much more in the spiritual realm. Heaven will be available to you!

One of the mindsets to come against is the one that says, "I have lots of rights." Remember what it says in Galatians 2:20—*"Nevertheless I live; yet not I, but Christ liveth in me"* (KJV).

Someone once came to me and said, "You keep talking about the same thing all the time." Until I come into the fullness of the Lord Jesus Christ, I am okay with that. It is on purpose that we are dead. It is no longer I that liveth. If you are breathing, there is a strong potential that you have been wounded or offended. It doesn't matter what happens in your life. What matters is what you do with what happens in your life.

I don't want to minimize what you have to walk through. People see me preach the Word and think that I am on cloud nine. The truth is that I live by the Spirit of the Lord, but the kingdom is definitely opposed, even in my own life. Our nature is in opposition to the Lord, and we must apply that understanding daily.

The foundational key that will push past the fundamental error in your life is God's attribute of love. Love is the only thing that will get you past the fundamental flaw that stops you from experiencing the fullness of heaven. You came from dirt and you are going back to dirt. Basically, you are just dirt without Christ. I do not mean to be offensive, but this is a reality. Without Christ, we are indeed absolutely nothing.

Many think that they themselves are worthy of salvation, but other people we know or interact with are not. We think, "That person is so evil and bad that they are not worthy." That is a lie from the pit of hell.

> Now a man came up to Jesus and asked, "Teacher, what good thing must I do to get eternal life?"
>
> "Why do you ask me about what is good?" Jesus replied. "There is only One who is good. If you want to enter life, obey the commandments." (Matthew 19:16–17, NIV)

We need to get over ourselves. Many times in a Christian community, people want me to line up with their way of thinking and side with them on specific issues. I am not the judge! Yes, there a judgment is coming, but I am not the judge of people. People want me to take their side in a disagreement. I show people the error of their ways, not anyone else's. If you pass judgment on one, you need to pass it on all. It is about your attitude and your heart position in all of it. I may feel sorry for you, but the key is where your heart is in it, and what is being produced in your life. The error in thinking is that somehow we need to be right by what we do. No, we are in right standing by the blood of the Lamb, which propels you to obey Him!

I know that God is on your side. We can't get through everything that bombards us unless we access more of the Lord. It's all about love. The biggest challenge to getting more data from God, and more revelation of a manifested heaven in your life, is getting more of the "'love walk." It is not just a nice statement to say, "For God so loved the world." We may think some people are unworthy of that, but guess what? You are unworthy. It is through the unmerited favour of God that the Lord chose you before the foundation of the world. He saw something in you that you may not have seen in yourself.

What fruit are you producing? If it isn't love, it isn't God. So many times we see the opposite of those things going on around us in this world. You are called to be His beacon of light. I believe it grieves the heart of God, and therefore it should grieve you when the opposite of love happens. I don't want to minimize what people go through, but it is time to come into the fullness of the Gospel. There are mysteries and secrets that the Lord desires to release and we need to walk through this stumbling block. We need to come against religious mindsets that make us believe that somehow we are better than someone else, that their sin is greater than ours, or that they are not worthy of love. Those are religious mindsets and those strongholds are coming down by the Spirit of the Lord. I can't bring them down. I can teach on it, but you need to catch it.

Luke 13: The Parable of the Pharisee and the Tax Collector

To some who were confident of their own righteousness and looked down on everyone else, Jesus told this parable: [10]"Two men went up to the temple to pray, one a Pharisee and the other a tax collector. [11]The Pharisee stood by himself and prayed: 'God, I thank you that I am not like other people—robbers, evildoers, adulterers—or even like this tax collector. [12]fast twice a week and give a tenth of all I get.' [13]"But the tax collector stood at a distance. He would not even look up to heaven, but beat his breast and said, 'God, have mercy on me, a sinner.' [14]"I tell you that this man, rather than the other, went home justified before God. For all those who exalt themselves will be humbled, and those who humble themselves will be exalted." (Luke 18:9–14, NIV)

If you are confident in your own righteousness, you look down on everybody else. The Lord Jesus made a way for you. He made it for everyone. One of the things that won't let you get past that database into the heavenly realm is your own righteousness. There is none that is righteous other than the Lord. Someone once said to me, "You are a good person." I responded and said, "I am a person with Christ in my life. Without him I can do nothing."

Paul said he is the worst of sinners. I am like Paul. I am not doing this by my righteousness. I do it by His righteousness. I can't walk out my righteousness; I walk it out by Him in my life. I don't care how much you know, unless you know it through the love of the Lord. If it is to puff you up and make you look good, forget about it. You need to have the love of the Lord. We often put the plank in everyone else's life and the speck in ours.

The Old Testament is about following rules and regulations, while The New Testament is about the attitude of the heart—without the grace of God, you cannot walk out the New Testament. The Lord looked favourably on the sinner. Jesus came for sinners; He came to set captives free. You can't think badly about a sinner, for that is not God's thinking. His thinking is, "I am going to touch him or her and get them on fire for me." We are all sinners and have fallen short of the glory of God. The free gift of God is eternal life in Christ Jesus.

I recently had a conversation with my son and he brought up love and humility, and that without these attributes we are just clanging cymbals. What propels you to a manifested heaven in your life? It is love and humility! Don't think for a second that you cannot stumble or fall. Once you think that way, you have already started to stumble and fall.

My wife Cathryn had a dream about someone who thought they had a lot of authority. They were on a train and the person started to wrestle with the devil. They were confident they would be able to throw the devil off the train. In reality, the opposite happened. It is a warning to all of us. When we think we are so good, the devil will use that thought against us. I would rather be like the tax collector than the Pharisee from Luke 18. Love and humility are the keys.

Some people are trying to hold other people down, to bind them. But the Lord says:

> Whatever you bind (declare to be improper and unlawful) on earth must be what is already bound in heaven; and whatever you loose (declare lawful) on earth must be what is already loosed in heaven. (Matthew 16:19)

You need to loose people of the things you are binding them with. You may think you are good and someone around you is not, because they have offended or wounded you. The Lord Jesus said there is not one who is good. All things work for good for those who believe in Christ Jesus. If there isn't a release of love, it isn't God; it is something else.

I am passionate about this, because we are coming into an age where nothing else is going to cut it. You need more of Him, not more of the world. There will be no one overshooting heaven; however, we have the potential of undershooting. You cannot be fanatical enough about the principles of the Lord Jesus. We need to get more fanatical. I come into contact with people everyday who know they are sinners and don't have a way out. I have a way out for them, and it is through the Lord Jesus Christ. Get ready for the explosion! The question is, will you be used in releasing the explosion on this earth, or are you going to bind people? That is the key.

> When the crowds heard this, they were astonished at his teaching. Hearing that Jesus had silenced the Sadducees, the Pharisees got together. One of them, an expert in the law, tested him with this question: "Teacher, which is the greatest commandment in the Law?"
>
> Jesus replied: "'Love the Lord your God with all your heart and with all your soul and with all your mind.' This

is the first and greatest commandment. And the second is like it: 'Love your neighbor as yourself.' All the Law and the Prophets hang on these two commandments." (Matthew 22:33–40, NIV)

Jesus always loved to silence the religious mindsets. My ministry is called to doing the works of Jesus. If I am not shaking the heavenlies and shaking mindsets, I am not doing what the Lord has called me to do. I am here to shake the heaven—and to shake you. I love you enough to shake you. In the scripture, the Sadducees and the Pharisees put their thinking together and something happened. I think they were a little ticked at Jesus. They thought, *Who is He to tell me that I am doing something wrong?* The process of opening your heart is not a common thing. When you open your heart to the correction of the Lord, it is a precious thing. There is not one who is perfect. I know one who is, and that is the Lord Jesus Christ. He has intervened and brought correction so many times in my life, and He wants to do the same for you. Will you allow Him? We don't have to understand it, but we must embrace His Word to walk under an open heaven in our lives.

You cannot love God and not love your neighbour. It is easy for us to see the speck in others' lives. You may even be thinking, *I know someone that needs to hear that.* No. *You* need to hear it! There is a fundamental flaw in my computer. All the data is there, and I have been a Christian thirty-six years, but I can't get access to it without getting by this fundamental error. You will continue to make that error if you can't get by the "love thing." You will never have access to the fullness of God in your life. Yes, you will be going to heaven, but you won't have access into the realms of glory and mysteries and secrets of the kingdom that He desires to release for your life. I cannot do anything without Him, but He has made a way for you to do it.

> See to it that no one falls short of the grace of God and that no bitter root grows up to cause trouble and defile many. (Hebrews 12:15, NIV)

A bitter root will cause trouble and defile many. I purpose not to talk about anybody's sin to anybody else; rather, I purpose to do that in my life. It is so easy to say, "Look what that person did! I am so hurt, wounded, and offended." We all have that potential. I will say, "Don't talk to me about what that person did. Talk to me about your heart and the attitude of your heart through what that person did." Every issue of life flows out of your heart. One of the individuals I am accountable to from eastern Canada handles it like this: if someone is speaking badly about him or belittling him, he sows financially into them. I mentioned to him one time, "When I am short of cash, I am going to hit you up."

> Love does not delight in evil but rejoices with the truth. ⁷It always protects, always trusts, always hopes, always perseveres. ⁸Love never fails. But where there are prophecies, they will cease; where there are tongues, they will be stilled; where there is knowledge, it will pass away. (1 Corinthians 13:6–8, NIV)

After sin was revealed in a person's life I knew, someone once came to me and said, "I prophesied this over that person a year ago. I knew they had sin in their lives! Aha! I knew it, I knew it."

"I don't want to hear about that," I said to them.

Everyone has sin in their lives; you do not have to be prophetic to see it. It is in our nature to sin. In this particular case, that person wanted me to edify their gift over someone else's life. A soul's eternal destiny rests in the balance, so let us ensure that we minister out of the atmosphere of heaven. If our words aren't rooted in love, it is the opposite of love. Don't put your prophetic gift above love. Love never fails. When you sow love, it will never fail. It may look like it did at times, but the Bible says that love never fails. If it isn't love, it isn't God.

> Then he told this parable: "A man had a fig tree growing in his vineyard, and he went to look for fruit on it but did not find any. [7] So he said to the man who took care of the vineyard, 'For three years now I've been coming to look for fruit on this fig tree and haven't found any. Cut it down! Why should it use up the soil?' [8] "'Sir,' the man replied, 'leave it alone for one more year, and I'll dig around it and fertilize it. [9] If it bears fruit next year, fine! If not, then cut it down.'" (Luke 13:6–9, NIV)

Here is a fig tree in the midst of a vineyard, and it is out of place. It is using resources and eating up all the profits of the vineyard. It goes down and takes all the nutrients intended for the grapes. Somebody owns this land. The owner is the Father. God has two attributes—mercy and judgment. God is a God of mercy, but also judgment. Sinners will be judged, and sin will be judged. The Bible is clear about that.

You can only approach the Lord in holiness. That holiness became available to you after Jesus paid for it at the cross. Something is happening in this scripture: mercy and judgement is being worked out. Maybe you know someone who you haven't seen fruit from in years. I am not the judge, and you are not the judge, either. We like to think that sinners won't be judged, but sinners *will* be judged. But not by me. Here is the Lord saying, "Leave it alone." The Lord desires to put manure around the tree, and around our lives. Do you have manure in your life? What is that manure intended for? Manure is used to fertilize you and produce fruit, so don't despise the manure. It produces love, mercy, and compassion. I need a little manure, which springs out of the issues of life. The manure produces something for your life. In the scripture, Jesus, the attribute of mercy, says that He is looking for more fruit, but He is going to give it more time. This is mercy being extended where there should have been judgement.

Sooner or later, the Lord will say, "Time's up." I don't know when, but I do know judgment is coming, and it starts in the house of the Lord. My gift is mercy. I will keep giving mercy, because I don't want judgment for you or me. I want His mercy. The act of extending love, mercy, compassion, and grace others will always produce a manifested heaven for you. It isn't about being right or wrong; it is about lining up your heart with the Lord's. So many times, I see believers condemning their brothers and sisters when they have sin in their own lives. I believe this grieves the heart of the Lord. Mercy is better than judgement. Will sin be judged? Absolutely, and I weep over people's lives, knowing that the Lord has a better way for them. Choose love and mercy to have heaven manifest in your life.

We have a very hard time coping when someone doesn't love us; when this happens, we simply don't know what to do. Many times, we become wounded and offended. Consequently, we think we are more spiritually mature than we really are. No matter what the atmosphere is, we must react out of a heart of love to get heavenly results. If it isn't love, it isn't God. When something comes at you that is in opposition to the love you are releasing, how do you respond? However you respond, you need to remember the words of Matthew 7:2—*"For in the same way you judge others, you will be judged, and with the measure you use, it will be measured to you"* (NIV).

A few years ago, I went out shooting bows and arrows with two of my sons, Tim (my older) and Jonathan (my youngest). Early one morning, after much practise, we went hunting. We set up a tree stand just on the fringe of a wallow. (A wallow is a place in the forest where wildlife comes to eat, drink, and relax; there is an abundance of vegetation and water there.) There was snow on the ground, and it was cold. We were trying to hunt white tail deer.

Animals can sense a human by their smell; they can hear everything, so we were being very quiet and every effort was made not to disturb the natural habitat. Every once in a while, we would hear a crack. Something in the wild was stepping on a twig and we would think our kill was coming quickly towards us.

By the end of the day, though, we hadn't seen any animals, so we started driving home. As we were driving, we were trying to determine why we hadn't seen any animals.

Tim piped up and said, "Well, I did pee in the wallow when I got there. Do you think that would have any effect on animals?"

"What! You did what?" I said. "You went pee in the wallow? Animals can sense the scent of humanity far away."

You may be wondering how this applies to the point I'm making. Well, here it is: don't pee in the wallow when it comes to love. In other words, if you have been called to a lifestyle of love, don't pee in the wallow to prevent that lifestyle from manifesting in your life. Do everything in advance to determine that you will not disturb the habitat of love before a needed situation comes upon you.

When we talk about love, you will be challenged in love. I had calls this week from people saying, "I love these people, but I am going to do this or that to them." Doing those things would be totally contrary to the will of the Lord. I laugh, because we let "pee in the wallow" dictate how we are going to respond. It is not what people do to you; it is what you do with it.

It is time to take ground on love. Everybody needs to be loved. Everybody has felt unloved. The Lord doesn't require a lot of words; He requires a lot of love. Every time I speak that out verbally, I am brought to the point of tears. Somehow we think we are better than most. I have the gift of prophesy, and I often see people with wounds that have been afflicted by others. You cannot have the concept of "us four and no more." We cannot pick out certain things about someone and not like them because of it. You need to love people. You are going to be challenged in it. You will be challenged to love. The best thing to do is determine in advance to walk the love walk, because we have been mandated to do it. Keep your mouth shut until you can walk in love!

When everything looks hopeless, love. Step back and apply love. Don't apply your emotions. The responsibility of love rests with each and every one of us. It rests with you and me. The level of your walk with the Lord directly reflects your level of love. When your love level goes up, so does your relationship with the Lord. It is not just the nice looking people you have to love. This is the Gospel. Everything is summed up that way. If you can't love people, you do not love God. The level of your relationship with Him is determined by love.

In my secular job, one of my supervisors was an alcoholic. He woke up and was consumed with getting that addiction satisfied by lunch. What are you consumed by? If it isn't love, it isn't God. When you wake up, despite what is going on around you, you need to determine that you are going to walk in a loving, Godly way. That is what determines the outcome of your relationship with the Lord. You can't touch Him unless you love people. I am a lover, not a fighter. The level of your relationship with Him is proportional to your level of love.

There is a collision coming, and it has already started. There are many who choose not to walk in love. Remember that it is not what happens to you; it is what you do with what happens to you. Everybody has been hurt. What are you doing with it? Don't waste your hurts. Purpose to lay down your life and get lower still by preferring others over yourself through your love walk.

What do you do in an abusive situation? You love your abuser, but you go to the authorities. Hear from the Lord, but still love. I am not trying to get you on a path to be beat up all the time. Your thoughts and attitude are absolutely important to your destiny. Does anybody follow hockey? Tom Renney, the coach of Edmonton Oilers, was quoted in the *Edmonton Sun* as saying, "When the going is easy, everybody glides along. Nobody gets tested. You never really find out what a guy really has in him, and hopefully it is good." If your love is not tested, you never really know what you have.

I will be preaching on love forever, until the fullness of the Lord comes. Many times we try and go another route, one other than love. Back in the Garden, Eve's sin stemmed from the emotional realm of her soul, as her desire to choose the forbidden fruit was in direct contradiction to God's Word. What was man's sin? He chose the women over God. Adam sinned, too. Eve was deceived. Adam knew what to do, but he chose the woman over God. These two things still plague men and women today. You can't apply emotions to the truth in the Word. There is only one truth; man started to apply his natural sense to a spiritual reality. Have you been hurt by someone? You cannot apply your emotions to the Gospel of love. You cannot apply your emotions to the will of God. It's like mixing water and oil. What becomes the truth? If you want to walk in the realm of God manifesting heaven in your life, you cannot be influenced by your emotions. I see this happen time and time again.

Don't be afraid of trench warfare. Have you ever heard of Pork Chop Hill? This was a hill in the Korean War that had trenches. The Chinese controlled it during negotiations at the end of the war, but the American's controlled it after they then counterattacked. A point was being made. Both sides were vying for it. The Chinese were determined to take it back from the Americans, and the Americans said, "Why do you want it? It means nothing, it is insignificant. Lives are being killed and destroyed. You know we will come to a peace agreement." The reason they were doing it was that the enemy was trying to make it a point of supremacy. You cannot be influenced by your emotions. The Americans realized what was going on, so they brought reinforcements and maintained that hill at all costs. Then the negotiations ended.

I tell you this because you can't negotiate with the devil. He wants you to be defeated and disappointed, but love never, ever fails. It is not rooted in emotion; it is rooted in the Word of God. When all hell comes against you and you want to slap somebody around, remember that you are seated far above principalities, powers, and rulers of darkness. Keep your position. The second you walk away from love is the second you go under.

CHAPTER TWENTY-ONE

Conclusion

As I was finishing this book, the Lord brought me open visions on two consecutive Mondays in our church's morning prayer time. I believe these visions are critical to our understanding of walking in the realm of a manifested, open heaven for our lives. Both of these visions, I believe, are upon us, and the choice is ours as to whether we walk in them or walk in a different direction. I also believe that a manifested heaven is completely about Him and what He is releasing on the earth today. I declare an open and manifested heaven for your life. Without Him, we can do nothing. The scriptures declare that we were created for Him and that everything exists for Him. This is, indeed, a mystery and a secret that is being released today for those who believe. It is definitely for you. Here are the visions in the format the Lord gave them to me:

Vision #1

During morning prayer on Monday, November 15, 2010, I felt such a strong and pronounced presence of the Lord that everyone in the room could not help but notice Him at work. Quite literally, He flooded into our sanctuary with the heavenly hosts and asked me this question: "Now that I am moving on the hearts of the lost, are you ready for a 24/7 revival to be released?

Honestly, my answer was, "No, I am not ready." Nor did I believe that our people were ready for such a move. I started to think about every practical aspect of how we could facilitate this move of the Spirit of the Lord.

Next, I felt the Lord say, "Lay down all these practicalities, because I am going to move on the hearts of the people and it will not be a work of the flesh, but of My Spirit."

I didn't have to put to be concerned for all the practicalities, because He was already moving on hearts and every aspect of revival would sovereignly be provided for under His complete direction.

Then a pronounced rest fell over my being like I have never experienced before. I believe it was a new measure of His manifested presence enveloping the complete sanctuary.

The Lord said that this move was for everyone who was thirsting and hungering for more of Him. His Spirit is sweeping over the complete earth, looking for a people to show Himself approved in (2 Chronicles 16:9). His Spirit is available to those who believe. These people and their regions have already been chosen and soon revivals of His presence will become common to His bride. Neither the world nor man will be able to contain it. The freshness of the Spirit is being released in a new way. The mysteries and secrets of His kingdom that have previously been hidden are now available, and a new illumination is coming to the scriptures as He releases new eyes to see and ears to hear. The dull of hearing and the short-sighted will see and hear clearly and the only thing required of them is the insatiable spiritual hunger that He is releasing for their hearts and lives.

My question to you today is the question the Lord posed to me: "Are you ready?"

We can all say yes, but are we truly ready? Because this move will cost us everything. The Lord is asking for our complete lives, not just bits and pieces and the crumbs of life, but it all. Surrendering ourselves to Him is everything. The question remains: are you ready? It will cost us everything. I believe the time is no. This is not a distant word. He is asking for your availability for His kingdom now! It has never been as close as it is today. My prayer is that you will receive this into your heart and ask yourself the same question I had to ask myself this morning. This is burning in me right now: His manifested presence will take you into a new realm of His glory. I believe that the Lord is removing every restriction right now, if you will let Him.

Vision # 2

In morning prayer on November 23, 2010, we experienced another strong visitation of the Lord. There is something about seeking the presence of the Lord that activates heaven!

I saw myself going into the inner court, the Holy of Holies, where I envisioned the Lord taking me into a heavenly place which He called it His portrait room. In this room, there were many portraits of the finest quality hanging on the walls. The room was not ordinary in size, but massive and able to accommodate thousands of people. In fact, there were thousands of people gathered around, all dressed in the finest garments—men in tuxedos and women in long, flowing gowns. The atmosphere was charged with electricity and I could see delight and great expectation on the faces of the people. Joy was evident everywhere!

Everyone was gazing at a portrait at one end of the room, even though the image was still covered by the whitest of fine linens. It was obvious that this portrait was to be shortly unveiled and had been carefully guarded and preserved. As the Lord Jesus began to walk towards the veiled portrait, legions of angels entered the room, and He began to radiate a heavenly whiteness that covered the room; the veiled portrait radiated the same light, even though it still remained veiled. The crowds of dignitaries fell flat on their faces and began to sing, "Holy, Holy, Holy is the Lamb!!!" It was obvious that something fresh was being released into the portrait room, something that was unprecedented in history. This was new and alive and empowering... it was like the light was bringing energy to the weary. A new dawning was definitely taking place.

The Lord Jesus then began to speak and He said this: "This work of Art has been saved for the last days and it is the greatest masterpiece that will ever be unveiled. Much work and preparation has been put into this work, but the unveiling is now upon us."

The dignitaries (some of whom I recognized from their accomplishments on earth) continued to sing while prostrate before Him, but the voice of the Lord superseded every other sound. His voice was filled with boldness and authority, and every word penetrated the atmosphere in the room. It was also evident that He was the artist whose greatest work was about to be unveiled. He went on to add that this masterpiece had never before been seen on the earth in such a great measure, although there had been brief peeks at it throughout history. This was to be a day of total release.

The timing, He said, was absolutely perfect. The work had been prepared for this exact time. When He said this, a new wave of intense praise was given up unto Him and there was a release of utter and complete unity in the room like nothing I have ever seen in my natural life here on earth. They began to worship and sing with abandon, not concerned with what was going on around them nut only concerned with the Lord and the unveiling that was momentarily upon them. The angelic beings smiled with great anticipation and expectation, realizing this was the day many had been waiting for and that they were present for the greatest unveiling in the history of humanity. Jesus savoured the moment, and it was obvious that He viewed this as His greatest achievement.

As the Lord carefully and with great confidence removed the fine linen from over the portrait, His radiance intensified, now focused totally and completely on every inch of the portrait with His greatest love. The only light in the room was now upon Him. The intensity increased twofold at this point and every eye was fixed on the unveiled portrait of the Lord's chosen bride. Heavenly praises from the great cloud of witnesses gathered there began to infuse the portrait. Everyone in the room began to declare with one voice, "What a masterpiece!" and "Look what the Lord has done!" Then the vision ended.

Upon reflecting on this vision, I have been so impressed about this fact and this fact alone—it is totally about Him and His masterpiece! He has painted it, He is satisfied with it, and the portrait is now released. Since receiving the vision, I have been overwhelmed by His presence, which emanates out of His goodness and love as demonstrated in the radiance of His portrait. There is nothing more beautiful in humanity! The bride, His bride, perfect in every detail, has been released. My natural understanding is that not everyone will be in the bride, but after seeing the portrait I am rethinking my position on this aspect and seeking the Lord on it, because He is the one doing the unveiling. I believe it His desire to see all called by His name to be part of His bride. It is upon us and I believe not one will be left out.

Dream

In the late evening of November 18, 2010, the Lord brought me into a three-part dream. In it, I saw myself from a position far above as I slept in a hospital bed. Two individuals, whom I perceived to be spiritual entities, were working on my feet as I slept. At first I could not discern whether they were doing something good or bad, but discernment hit me as they started to move up my legs. I was struck with the realization that what was happening was not good at all; these were dark entities sent to work against the body, starting with the feet. They were attempting to bring paralysis against the body, which would first render the body incapable of walking and then work to shut down every other organ as they moved upwards.

Suddenly I saw myself awake. At the instant of awakening, the beings had no authority to touch my body and they quite literally became paralysed themselves and only had the power to watch me. Next, I heard the voice of a close friend and former associate pastor—his name was Steve Rowe—and he was broadcasting a message of the hospital intercom, to the effect of, "Your ride is outside. Get up." So, with confidence and authority, I arose and walked down a long corridor to the main entrance of the hospital with, neither concern nor care for the entities who had previously been working on my feet.

At the main entrance, I was met by a man who was obviously in control of my ride, which was a Harley Davidson motorcycle. There was a beautiful woman sitting side-saddle. He indicated to me to get on the bike, in a position directly behind the woman. This was interesting. How in the world were all three of us going to ride on this motorcycle? Next thing I knew, the motorcycle was starting up and we were off on the ride of our lives. We came upon barrier after barrier; there were anywhere from fifteen to twenty of them. They all looked physically impossible to drive through in the natural, but the motorcycle passed through each barrier with ease, as if it was travelling through paper-thin material. Suddenly I also realized that the motorcycle was driverless and that the previous driver was operating it by remote control from a distance. He was carefully observing each and every barrier as we approached them, manoeuvring the motorcycle around them even as we picked up speed.

I believe that this dream has tremendous spiritual significance. First of all, is it possible for us to think we are awake when we are spiritually asleep? From this dream, the answer is obviously yes. Next, we need to spiritually discern that there are entities out there striving to bring paralysis to the body, starting with the feet. I also believe that the Lord is calling us out of a hospital environment, where Christians have for the most part found themselves for the better part of two thousand years. Finally, I believe the beautiful woman in my dream was the bride of Christ and that the driver was our risen Saviour, who was remotely taking us on the ride of our lives through each and every obstacle in our way. We are, indeed, living in exciting times, and my exhortation to you is to get ready for this ride, because it will be filled with excitement as we journey forward.

There it is. I believe that heaven on earth is available to us. As you pursue Him, His mysteries and secrets will draw you in deeper to the things He has for you. You will no longer be dictated to by the circumstances and situations of your life. These issues will no longer captivate your attention, but you will be totally consumed by His presence in your life! Remember this: you are totally and completely loved by Him in every way. See Him at work in your life!